101 WAYS TO SUCCESSFULLY MARKET YOURSELF

Jay Miletsky

Course Technology PTR

A part of Cengage Learning

COURSE TECHNOLOGY
CENGAGE Learning™

Australia, Brazil, Japan, Korea, Mexico, Singapore, Spain, United Kingdom, United States

COURSE TECHNOLOGY
CENGAGE Learning™

101 Ways to Successfully Market Yourself
Jay Miletsky

Publisher and General Manager, Course Technology PTR:
Stacy L. Hiquet

Associate Director of Marketing:
Sarah Panella

Manager of Editorial Services:
Heather Talbot

Marketing Manager:
Mark Hughes

Acquisitions Editor:
Mitzi Koontz

Project Editor:
Sandi Wilson

Editorial Services Coordinator:
Jen Blaney

Copy Editor:
Sandi Wilson

Interior Layout :
Jill Flores

Cover Designer:
Mike Tanamachi

Indexer:
Broccoli Information Management

Proofreader:
Sara Gullion

Course Technology, a part of Cengage Learning
20 Channel Center Street
Boston, MA 02210
USA

For product information and technology assistance, contact us at **Cengage Learning Academic Resource Center, 1-800-354-9706**

For permission to use material from this text or product, submit all requests online at **cengage.com/permissions**
Further permissions questions can be emailed to **permissionrequest@cengage.com**

All trademarks are the property of their respective owners.

All images © Cengage Learning unless otherwise noted.

Library of Congress Control Number: 2009939185

ISBN-13: 978-1-4354-5510-8

ISBN-10: 1-4354-5510-X

Cengage Learning is a leading provider of customized learning solutions with office locations around the globe, including Singapore, the United Kingdom, Australia, Mexico, Brazil, and Japan. Locate your local office at: **international.cengage.com/region**

Cengage Learning products are represented in Canada by Nelson Education, Ltd.

For your lifelong learning solutions, visit **courseptr.com**.

Printed in United States
2 3 4 5 6 7 11

*Cindi—I wouldn't have finished
this without your help.*

ACKNOWLEDGMENTS

I'd like to thank everyone at Cengage Learning, especially Mitzi Koontz, for all of their work and for continuing to give me the opportunity to write for them.

About the Author

Jay Miletsky is CEO and executive creative director of Mango (formerly PFS Marketwyse), a leading marketing communications agency in the New York Metro area. His marketing work has included successful consultation and campaigns for companies including Hershey's, AmerisourceBergen, Emerson Electric, JVC, The Michael C. Fina Company and more. Miletsky is a featured speaker for numerous companies and seminars as well as a guest lecturer for universities. He is the author of 10 books, including *Perspectives on Marketing* and *Perspectives on Branding*, and blogs regularly at jaymiletsky.com and getperspectives.com. You can follow him on Twitter at http://twitter.com/jaymiletsky.

CONTENTS

Part II
Make the Most of the Web

Part III
There's Life Offline—Get Out and Meet Real People 35

x   Contents

INTRODUCTION

With more than six billion people in the world, you wouldn't think it would be very hard to just go out and meet some of them. But it can be tough. Even crowded rooms can be lonely places if you don't know how to initiate contact with others. It's not easy. Meeting new people means putting yourself out there and risking rejection—a fate that everyone would rather avoid.

But with great risk comes the opportunity for great reward, and if you market yourself correctly, there's no limit to what you can accomplish.

- **Find a job.** Maybe you're right out of school and suddenly find yourself out in the real world (sorry, no more 11:00am classes and beer for breakfast). Maybe you've long since graduated and now find yourself in a boring, dead-end job and want something better. Maybe you've suddenly been downsized from your comfortable position mid-career, and it's time to put your many contacts to work for you as you find a new job. Whatever your motivation for your job search, you're going to need to get out there and meet the right people.

- **Sell something.** Sales people rarely find success sitting at home and watching TV. Sales is a tough road that requires getting to know a lot of people and getting them to believe in you and buy into your product or service. For sales people, marketing yourself comes with the territory, and the ones who master these skills will win.

- **Promote your own company.** Entrepreneurs have to wear a lot of hats. The statistics show that more often than not, very few new businesses will survive past the first few years. Along with everything else they have on their plate, business owners need to be out there and get themselves seen and known. If you're an entrepreneur, very often you are the business, so marketing yourself is equivalent to marketing your business.

- **Grab a piece of the spotlight.** With the growth of cell phone and computer cameras, along with the explosion of YouTube, many individuals are anxious to be the next "cyberlebrity." But the online fame that comes from a single popular video is usually fleeting, and afterward you're back to being an unknown, your 15 minutes of fame cut tragically short. More long-term fame, however, as a thought leader or innovator in your industry, can come from strategically and consistently marketing yourself.

- **Make some new friends.** If you're still in college, you probably won't believe me, but making new friends after graduation is way harder than it was in school. The same outlets of classes and clubs and cramped living conditions simply don't exist after school is over, and with it goes many of the social opportunities you've come to count on for meeting new people. It's possible you don't necessarily want a new job, fame, or to sell anything, but you just want some outlets to meet new people, make some friends, and maybe go on a date or two. Marketing yourself will certainly help in these areas as well.

As you can see, there are many ways to reach success though self-promotion and marketing oneself. Whatever your goals are, there's absolutely no reason why, with a little knowledge and effort, you can't reach and surpass them.

The trick is to have fun. Those who consider marketing themselves to be a chore probably would be better off putting this book down, grabbing a pint of ice cream, and settling in for the night, alone. The fact of the matter is that if you consider marketing yourself to be a job, there's really no way to be consistently or believably good at it. Sure, maybe you'll make a few new connections here and there, but that's really not what marketing yourself is about—and it's certainly not what this book is about! Successfully marketing yourself is about loving the process—being more of an extrovert and enjoying the process of meeting new people. The more you enjoy it, the more fun you have with it, the more successful you'll be.

In writing this book I have, as best as possible, tried to give specific advice as it pertains to networking, while remaining aware that different readers will have different reasons for wanting to market themselves. You'll pick up suggestions on how to present yourself and relate to others, how to find the right audiences, and how to expand your network both online and off. In *101 Ways to Successfully Market Yourself*, I've provided you with advice from my own experience, organized in a series of tips that are both philosophical and practical (actually, there are far more practical and tactical tips in this book than philosophical ones).

I hope this book will help you make a lot of new and useful contacts. To start you off, I offer myself as your first new connection.

Follow me on Twitter: @jaymiletsky

Enjoy the book, and good luck in your campaign to market yourself!

PART I

27 MYMs
(MARKETING-YOURSELF-MANDATES)

I f you get nothing else out of this book at all—you're simply flip-ping through the pages at the store with no real intention to buy, or will likely use it to steady a wobbly chair long before you get a chance to finish it—read this section carefully. The 27 Marketing-Yourself-Mandates (what I refer to as the 27 MYMs) will establish the foundation of your self-promotional efforts.

1: Understand Your Personal Brand

Most likely, you're familiar with the term "brand" as it applies to prod-ucts, services, or companies. Pepsi, Apple, Nike—these and others like them are all recognizable brand names that we use everyday. But are people brands? Are *you* a brand? In order to answer that, we first need to do a quick review about what a brand actually is.

Many people incorrectly believe that a brand is simply a logo. It's not. A logo is *part* of a brand—the part that helps consumers recognize the product, service, or company that it represents. But the brand itself is intangible; and can be defined as:

> Brand: The sum total of all user experiences with a particular product, service, or company, building both reputation and future expectations of benefit.

In short, the brand is a reputation. If a product has a good reputation, there's a greater likelihood consumers will want to buy it. If it had a bad reputation, there's less likelihood consumers will want to buy it. The same basic tenet holds true for people, as well. Your personal brand is your personal reputation. What do people think of you? What do they expect from you? Are you someone they'll want to be associated with, or someone they want to distance themselves from? These decisions and more will be made as people learn more about you, and take in all aspects of your personality, sense of style, unique qualities, what you say, how you say it, whether or not you follow through on your commitments, and what you potentially bring to the table. Your personal brand is central to your success in marketing yourself and sustaining relevant, long term connections, so keep it in mind at all times and at all costs.

2: Know the Clichéd Basics

Part of me wishes I could skip these altogether, because they're overdone to the extent of being hackneyed. But they do have some merit, so I'm lumping the basics into a single mandate with minimal (or no) explanation for each item:

- Look people in the eye when you talk to them.
- Use a firm handshake.
- Exude confidence.
- You are what you eat. In other words, watch what you order when you network with people over lunch or dinner. Broccoli will get between your teeth and ribs are just messy.
- Dress for success. No, that doesn't (necessarily) mean you have to dust off the tux and prepare for the prom. It means to dress appropriately for your industry. If you're in a fairly conservative field, such as law or accounting, well, you might need to break out the blazer and tie. If you're in a more creative field, such as music or advertising, then more casual clothes are fine. Dress the part.
- Always have a Tic-Tac handy. Bad breath is never a good way to start a conversation. Basic rule to remember: if someone offers you a piece of gum, take it—they might be offering it for a reason.
- Be polite and remember the standard etiquette we all learned in grammar school.
- Make your first impression your best impression.

3: Be Happy!

Don't start marketing yourself if you're in the mindset that life sucks, you never have any good opportunities come your way, there are always dark clouds looming. A big part of marketing yourself is mastering the art of personal attraction. In general, people are attracted to positive attitudes. I'm not advocating you fake it—pretending to be positive is usually pretty obvious, and anybody paying even a little bit of attention will see right through you. What I'm advocating is that you genuinely be happy! Now please don't run off and buy a new copy of *The Secret*, but I honestly believe that people can train themselves to be more positive, and view their life and situations in a more constructive light. When problems or issues come up, do you concentrate on finding ways to solve them, or do you sulk and take a "woe is me" attitude? Does negativity help give you definition and purpose? I could go on and on about this one topic, but the bottom line is that whatever your situation is, find the best in it, be focused, and be happy. Positive actions breed positive results.

4: Be Yourself

There's a big difference between being who you actually are, and who you want to be. Play acting the character that doesn't come naturally to you is not only exhausting, it's obvious, and people will turn off to you as soon as they realize you're not being genuine.

The reason why so many people struggle with this particular point is that the world gives so much attention to the loud and obnoxious. Perez Hilton, Britney Spears, Lindsay Lohan—seems the more people misbehave, the more attention they get. So it makes sense that in an effort to increase their own visibility, many people will try to adopt louder personalities. But there are two things to remember:

- First, chances are, Perez Hilton doesn't have to try all that hard to be obnoxious—my guess is that it comes pretty naturally to him. He's just being himself, rather than being a made-up character.

- Second, being obnoxious isn't the only way to increase one's profile. While there's not a lot of room in marketing for shy and quiet, there are plenty of opportunities for being successful by being the hero rather than the villain.

So who are you? That question shouldn't be too difficult to answer. Be real. Be comfortable. And just be yourself.

5: Talk Less and Do More

Dreaming is easy, which is why dreamers are a dime a dozen. The problem is that years from now, dreamers won't have much to show for their dreams except disappointment. Doers, on the other hand, take dreaming to the next level, and work to actually make success a reality.

I've written a lot of books over the years (I believe this is my tenth). And every time I start writing one, new people tell me with total sincerity, "Oh! I was thinking about writing a book, too!" As though it's just that easy: I simply snap my fingers, and the words magically appear on the page. The fact of the matter is, none of these people actually want to write a book. What they want and what they dream about is seeing their name on the cover, seeing their book in a bookstore, telling people about the book they wrote, and signing copies of it for people they've never met. But they don't want to go through the real work of actually *writing* one of these. Writing a book is not easy. It's a nightmare, to be brutally honest. It's isolating; it's mind numbing; it's stressful; and it takes you away from spending time with friends and family. Most people don't want to go through all that— it's far easier to just tell people that you want to write a book, and enjoy any small bit of praise that might come from that.

Don't fall into that trap of playing corporate exec, or talking too much about everything you want to accomplish. If you want something, go do it. Put the work in. Achieve success rather than allude to it.

6: Set a Goal—Market Yourself with a Purpose

Why do you want to market yourself? Clearly, sitting on the couch and watching cheesy VH1 reality shows is a lot easier and a lot more relaxing, so what is it you're looking to accomplish? There has to be a goal you're shooting for. Whether it is to land a new job, find a date, make new friends, improve your sales, find fame within your industry, or some other reason, make sure you have a clear goal to shoot for. Without the goal, you'll never be able to forge the right path, and you could end up running in circles.

7: Listen First, Talk Second

On the one hand, nobody likes a blowhard who dominates the conversation. Nothing is more boring. On the other hand, people love to hear themselves speak, and will take any opportunity they can to wax poetic on their life story, experiences, and opinions. Put both hands together, and you've got a very simple rule: listen first, talk second. Giving people a platform to talk will help endear them to you, and make them want to interact more with you in the future—where there will be plenty of time to talk about yourself.

8: Ask Questions and Find Common Ground

Finding common ground is one of the best ways of turning a connection into an opportunity. It makes it easier to forge deeper inroads and maintain contact. So get to know as much about everyone as you can, and see where the common ground lies. Ask questions—where are they from? What do they do? Where did they go to school? Are they into sports, and if so, what teams do they follow? Where did they grow up? I'm not saying to shine a spotlight on people and grill them like you're trying to solve a murder case; just be inquisitive enough to see where deeper connections lie.

9: Approach Without Fear—People Don't Bite

Possibly the biggest roadblock to success in self-marketing is the inability to approach other people. Even at networking events where attendees are there to meet other people, there are those who will stay near the bar, talking only with the people they went there with, too shy to approach anyone that they don't know.

Well, puff up your chest, put a smile on, and get ready to shake a few hands—it's what self promotion is all about. There's really nothing to be afraid of. Usually, if you say "hi" and introduce yourself, people will smile and introduce themselves back. People don't bite.

10: Don't Waste Time

It's amazing how many people think they can't get ahead or do the things they want to do in life because they "never have enough time."

Not true! People waste more time than they know what to do with, usually in ways we don't even realize.

I had a friend years back that called me around 8:00 p.m. one night during the week, complaining that she had at least three hours worth of work to do that night, and she'd never catch up, and she didn't know how she'd get it all done. About an hour later, I finally interrupted and said, "We've been on the phone an hour, and my guess is that I'm not the first person you called tonight. If I'm the third, and you spent an hour complaining to each of us, that's three hours right there. You could have been done with your work by now." Obviously, she didn't appreciate me pointing that out, but people rarely want to hear the truth. The fact of the matter is most people waste a lot of time without ever realizing it. Marketing yourself can be a time consuming process, so use your time wisely and waste as little time as possible.

11: Have Something Unique to Contribute

So, what are you bringing to the party? What do you have, say, or know that's going to make you stand out, and make people want to connect and stay connected? If you want to stand out, you need to be unique—offer some insight, knowledge, creativity, experience, angle, service, product, or wisdom that people will be interested in and unable to find elsewhere.

12: Don't Complain – Nobody Wants to Hear It

When someone asks, "How are you?" they want you to say, "Fine, thanks. How are you?" Nobody's interested in hearing about your jerk of a boss, the pain in your lower back that won't go away, or how you're dreading your next birthday. That's just a drag, and won't do anything but push people away. Save the griping for close friends and family, and put on a happy face for everyone else.

13: You Can't Just Be Selling

Whatever your reasons are for marketing yourself, it can't be all about you. Any relationship takes a certain amount of give and take, so as much as you may want to be out there selling yourself, you're going to have to exercise some restraint and see what other people's needs are, and look for ways to help them reach their goals. Or just shoot an e-mail every now and then just to say hello, showing that you value people for reasons other than work. Over time, helping people with seemingly selfless acts or just being friendly will come back to pay dividends in the future. I'm not talking about karma— I'm talking about the basic truism that people will usually go out of their way to help those who have helped them.

14: Take a Compliment, but Stay Humble

Strike a balance between being proud of yourself and your accomplishments, and being humble. Humility is an attractive quality that reflects confidence, but don't let it overshadow your talents and experience. Too much of anything—pride or humility—is not a good thing.

15: Don't Offend or Alienate

Religion and politics are always volatile issues, and can create lines of division that are difficult to get past. People often take both topics very personally, and get easily offended if they feel that their opinions and beliefs are being attacked. Keep that in mind, and remember that no matter how firm you are in your convictions, others may not agree. So be careful not to offend with what you feel is nothing more than a casual addition to a conversation. For example, consider the following:

New Contact: So how's business been?

Marketer: Not bad… you know, the President's doing everything he can to raise our expenses, but we're getting through.

Believe it or not, this kind of exchange happens very often. The marketer, so sure in his or her own belief, simply assumes that the new contact feels the same way. But that's not a guarantee, and if the new contact has a different viewpoint, then the conversation will either fall into an uncomfortable debate, or have an abrupt and awkward ending. Avoid this by simply avoiding politics or religion as a topic of conversation until you get to know individual contacts better and get a sense of whether or not these topics are safe to broach.

16: Stay Current

Conversation will play a central role in your marketing efforts. Better connections especially require deeper interaction than a simple greeting and handshake. Make sure you have plenty to talk about by keeping up to date and staying current with relative topics within your industry, news, sports, entertainment, and any other subjects your audience is likely to discuss.

17: Know Your Audience

It's not enough to simply say "I want to market myself" and head on out to the nearest public place with a friendly smile. Sure, you might meet some people that way, and you never know who may end up being a valuable contact in the future, but make the most of your time by concentrating your efforts on people that are more likely to be relevant to your goals. Think carefully about who your audience is, beyond generalities. It's not going to be enough to say "I want to market myself better within the legal community." That's too vague. Consider the average age of the people you want to meet, their gender, personality traits, outside interests, and so on. Knowing your audience will help you find them and relate to them more effectively.

18: Don't Treat People Like They're Inferior

When it comes to marketing yourself, the importance of confidence always comes up (it's so common, in fact, that I included it in my earlier list of clichéd basics). Too often, though, people find confidence in themselves by being condescending to others. No matter how smart you are, how many degrees you've earned, how much money you have, or what your ambitions are, you're not any better than anybody else. Don't treat anybody—waiters, parking garage attendants, valets, receptionists, interns, or anyone else like they don't matter or contribute. It just makes you look like a jerk. And nobody likes a jerk.

19: Opportunities Aren't Always Obvious

Don't give up on someone just because he or she might not directly be able to help you reach your goals. I don't want to sound like a Zen monk or anything, but the path to success in marketing yourself isn't always a straight line. You never know who other people know, and who they can put you in contact with.

I remember one day several years back, I was chatting with the woman who cuts my hair. I'd been going to her for years, and over that time we had chit-chatted about this and that and gotten to be friendly. She wasn't anyone who could give me or my marketing agency any business, but I'd keep her updated on some of the more interesting work my agency produced. Well, this one day, as I was telling her about a project I was particularly excited about, she said, "You know, I have a customer who's a marketing director at a pretty large company. I should tell her about you. Do you have an extra business card on you?" Within a month that marketing director and I had our first meeting, and about three months after that the company became our newest client. You just never know who people can put you in touch with.

20: Sharpen Your Speaking Abilities

We've all heard the statistics that, in general, people fear public speaking more than they fear death. But when it comes to marketing yourself, being able to speak (to an individual, small group, or large audience) isn't a suggestion, it's a requirement.

There are two parts of speaking that need to be considered:

- **Fear:** There's no question that speaking can be scary—especially if you're speaking to a group of people at once. I'm not a psychiatrist, but I believe that behind people's fear of speaking is fear of ridicule—fear that the audience will be bitingly critical of both our content and performance. But imagination is always stronger than reality, and the truth is, when you're speaking to people about a specific topic, they want you to succeed. They want to learn from what you're saying. And if they happen to be unhappy with what you're saying or how you're saying it, they'll still typically be polite about it and not bring you down. There's far less to be afraid of than you might think.

- **Clarity:** This is the one that I personally struggle with the most. Growing up, the question I heard people ask me most often was *"What?"* after almost anything I said. Apparently, my mind works crazy fast, and in my mouth's attempt to keep up, I speak so quickly that I slur all of my words to the point of being completely incoherent. So what's the point of speaking at all if nobody can understand a word you say? There are plenty of books you can buy that will teach you to be a better speaker, and of course you can always hire a coach to improve your speaking abilities, but before you do that, try these simple procedures

- Read out loud to somebody. It doesn't matter what you're reading—it could be a news article, fiction book, whatever—the important thing is that the person that you're reading to should be able to follow and understand the story. This will force you to read more slowly, and pay more attention to how you pronounce and annunciate each of your words.

- Give a speech or talk to yourself in the mirror. Watch your lips move, and make sure they are forming all of the words as you speak them.

- Don't be afraid to stop and pause between thoughts. A little silence is better than the unintentional "ummm" that often fills people's speech gaps.

- Speak into a digital recorder or video tape yourself speaking, and play it back for yourself. Chances are you'll be surprised by what you hear, and be able to pinpoint some of your specific problems.

21: Sharpen Your Writing Abilities

E-mail, blog posts, blog comments, white papers, speeches, resumes, books—writing is an everyday part of business and an integral part of marketing yourself. Learning to write well is key, and good authors will know how to use language and words to establish their voice and personality through words. If you plan on marketing yourself, you'll be doing a lot of writing, so get ready for it and learn to do it well. (Quick tip: If you want to write well, start reading. Being a reader is step one to being a good writer.)

22: Do Something Specific to Stand Out

As soon as you accomplish something that separates you from the crowd, you'll find yourself more in demand. Write a book, contribute articles to a popular print or online publication, or record a series of Web videos that get people's attention. Get your MBA, or better yet, your doctorate. Hold a seminar. Write a white paper on some industry issue.

If you have a more, um… "out there" personality, you could also take steps that are a little less conventional. In the past, there have been stories of newly graduated students who have printed their resume on their t-shirts, or even posted their picture and phone number on a highway billboard as a way of attracting attention. If you can come up with an original idea, you can put yourself in a pretty bright spotlight.

Whichever route you take, produce or accomplish something that shows you've attained some level of success and knowledge.

23: Ask for What You Want

There's never any harm in asking someone for what you want. Never assume that people you meet or market to will jump into action or know what you want if you don't ask them. There's nothing wrong with simply—and politely—asking for help, for work, or for someone to make a connection for you.

Of course, you need to approach this intelligently, so you'll have better luck getting the results you're looking for after establishing a relationship, showing interest in them, and demonstrating a willingness to help them out if and when you can.

24: Like It or Not, Appearance Counts

I'm not just talking about the clothes you wear, although your personal fashion style is definitely part of your overall appearance and can make an impact on your efforts to market yourself. What I'm really talking about is the elephant in the room of any conversation about marketing oneself: the fact that people are attracted to good looking people. I know it's not politically correct, but the fact of the matter is that there is a reason why most sales professionals, CEOs, and other people who have a public or extroverted business role are physically attractive. So put the cookie down, hit the gym, find a comb, apply some acne cream, grab some deodorant, and make a dental appointment. Be as attractive as possible—people will not only be more likely to approach you, but it'll increase your own confidence level, making it easier for you to approach other people.

25: Keep Contacts Constantly Organized

Not all contacts are created equal. Some are more valuable than others, some need more attention, and others aren't worth spending a lot of time on. As you meet more people, it can get confusing to keep them all straight. Keep all contacts organized from the outset. Whether you use ACT, Excel, or some other database, list each new contact into groups of "Hot," "Warm," and "Cold," with notes on who they are, what they do, how you met, any personal info about them, when you last contacted them, and what next steps (if any) you should take.

26: Keep Consistent

Remember the warning that Mr. Miyagi gave Daniel just before the training sequences began in *The Karate Kid*?

> Walk on road, hm? Walk left side, safe. Walk right side, safe. Walk middle, sooner or later <squish gesture> get squish just like grape.

> Here, karate, same thing. Either you karate do "yes" or karate do "no." You karate do "guess so," <squish> just like grape.

Well, what Mr. Miyagi probably didn't realize is that that memorable line applies every bit as much to marketing oneself as it does to walking down the street or learning karate. Self promotion isn't a practice that you can float in and out of, making yourself visible for a short while then disappearing for a time, resurfacing for a bit, then getting bored and giving up for awhile. It doesn't work that way. While work, family life, vacations, and other distractions will always threaten to take up more of your time, and emergencies can always popup and put a kink in your schedule, do your best to maintain a regular public presence and market yourself consistently.

27: Don't Give Up—It Won't Happen Overnight

Marketing yourself is a process, and a potentially frustrating one. It takes awhile to meet new people and build a following. Very often, the steps you take toward your goals won't always be obvious, and it won't feel like you're moving forward at all. You are. Keep that in mind and remember that building a network takes work, time, and perseverance. Giving up is a permanent solution to a temporary problem.

Part II

Make the Most of the Web

If you're one of those people who thinks you can still market yourself effectively without using the Web, guess again. Social networking may die down a bit over time, but it's here to stay—and it's an amazing opportunity to connect yourself with more people than you'd ever have a chance to meet in real-life. The trick is to really know how to make the most of the Web.

Unlike the other sections of this book, I'm going to break this up into subsections so I can give tips on how to use various tools individually. Please note: For the most part, the tips here will be how to use these tools for marketing yourself. While I'll spare a few words in certain areas to explain how one or more functions work, I unfortunately don't have the space to go into a full description of how to use Twitter, set up a blog, etc. If you don't already have a basic knowledge of how to use the social media outlets addressed here, I'd suggest finding a guide that explains it, and get to know them as quickly as possible.

Web Marketing in General

28: Make Social Networking Part of Your Daily Routine

So here's the thing about social networking: it can be time consuming and it can take awhile before you really start seeing results. This can be frustrating, because thanks to the speed of the Web, most people have lost their patience to allow things to happen over time. But it does take time and it does take effort. The trick is not to look at social media as a chore or something you need to get out of the way, but to adopt it as part of your lifestyle, as much a part of your daily routine as showering or brushing your teeth.

For example, my routine (and much of the following that will be discussed in greater detail later in the section) is to wake up each morning, turn on my laptop, and go to AdAge.com. I find an article I think is interesting and that I have an opinion on, and leave a long comment on it (I copy and paste my comment into a Word document and save it on my hardrive for later use). I then grab the URL for the article, shorten it using bit.ly, and broadcast it out through Twitter, Facebook, and LinkedIn. Throughout the day I try and find five new people to follow on Twitter and five new people to be friends with on Facebook. At least twice each week I respond to a post in a LinkedIn group that I subscribe to, and at least once each week I publish a new blog post (usually using one of the comments that I had left on AdAge.com throughout the week). Finally, I send an e-mail blast out to all of my contacts once per month, letting them know about new blog posts and other information.

Consider your daily schedule, and find a way to weave your online efforts into your everyday ritual to truly make the most of it.

29: Get to Know the "Big 3" But Look Beyond Them as Well

The "Big 3," at least at the time of this writing, are Facebook, Twitter, and LinkedIn. Now, that may change—social networks seem to have a tendency for gaining and losing favor without very much notice, but for the time being, these three are pretty important and are likely to play an important role in marketing oneself for some time. Learn how to use them as best as you can. Social networking, if done right, can put you in contact with many more people than you could possibly meet otherwise, and it will play a central role in your efforts.

While the Big 3 are arguably the most important networks for marketing yourself, the social media universe is a big place. There are plenty of other networks that are relevant as well, including Digg, Technorati, and an uncountable number specifically established to serve people interested in a specific industry or hobby. Focus on the Big 3 at the very least, but keep your eyes open and consider other networks that might help you reach your own personal goals.

30: Use an Avatar That Represents You Well

For those not familiar with the term, when it comes to computing, an avatar is an image (design, illustration, or photograph) that people or organizations use to represent themselves online. To maintain consistency and make yourself more recognizable, use the same avatar for all of the networks you get involved with, and make sure you choose one that represents you well. For the purposes of marketing yourself, I'd recommend using an easy-to-see, well taken head shot of yourself—one that shows off who you are, as well as your personality (serious, irreverent, artistic, etc.).

Twitter

31: Understand the Basic Concept

Twitter is a communication tool where people say anything they'd like in 140 characters or less. Although there are ways to have private conversations with one or more people on Twitter, by and large, Twitter is a public forum. Anything you write (or "tweet") will be sent out into the universe for anybody on the network to see. People can keep close track of what you have to say by "following" you, and similarly you can decide who you wish to follow and track more closely. Many people use it for sharing links to information they have written or have read and find interesting. It's a great platform for meeting people who share the same interests and industry as you, and eventually having influence over a great number of people.

32: Your Profile Matters

Before people follow you (at least, people who matter for your marketing purposes), they'll check out your Twitter profile, so make sure it's done well. Along with using an avatar that complements you (as discussed earlier), you should have an attractive background that represents your personality. (Twitter allows you to change the background of your page to one of their designs and color schemes, or you can upload your own.) You also need to have a brief but relevant bio that explains who you are and what you do or what you're interested in, so people can decide whether or not they want to follow your tweets. A thoughtful, well-crafted profile can gain you a lot of followers just as a poorly done profile can drive potential followers away.

33: Follow People First, and Make Sure They Matter

Unless you're already very well known (in which case, it's doubtful you'd need this book), people aren't going to race to start following you on Twitter. You need to make an effort first. Find people who seem to tweet about subjects you're interested in and that you'd like to connect with. Follow those people—they'll be alerted, and if they're interested in you (after looking at your profile and the quality of your tweets), they'll follow you back.

34: Be an Active Tweeter—One a Day Will Keep Followers Away

If you want to build a strong following on Twitter, you need to be active. You can't just go on in the morning, send a tweet out before breakfast and expect the followers to come flooding in. You need to stay active, and make yourself seen. More people will follow you if you appear more often, rather than just float on and off sporadically.

35: Don't Be Too Quick to Block Followers

Like any network, Twitter is filled with spammers, so expect to be followed by people who will try to sell you mail-order brides, get rich quick schemes, or online porn subscriptions. The natural instinct is to block these people from following you. Don't. Remember, as long as you don't follow them back, you can't read any of the junk that they write, and in the meantime, the more people you have following you, the more attractive you'll seem to other, more legitimate people who consider following you. If the spammers start to crowd you with tons of direct messages, then clearly you need to block them, but until then, there's no harm in having them bulk up your numbers.

36: Don't Just Sell—Send Quality Tweets and Show Your Human Side

In an odd way, there's a certain etiquette that most people on Twitter live by. Part of that etiquette is not to be too overly promotional. It turns people off. Nobody likes to feel pressured, and few people want to engage in conversations with people who are always trying to sell them something, so turn off the urge to make all your tweets about things you make, write, speak about, or market. As a rule, I'd say that it's usually acceptable to be self-indulgent one out of every five tweets. In between, mix in information that will both attract people and show that you're a real person and not just some sales-robot. For example:

Tweet 1: Self-promotional

Tweet 2: Link to an article on the Web that you find interesting

Tweet 3: Something fun or personal

Tweet 4: Re-tweet someone else's message

Tweet 5: Link to an article on the Web that you find interesting

Tweet 6: Self-promotional

They don't have to necessarily be in that order, of course. The point is just to try and mix it up a little. Making your tweets about something other than yourself and what you're trying to accomplish will make it more likely that people will want to follow you.

37: Stay Consistent

Keep your tweets within your area of interest. You'll be more likely to build a following of potentially useful connections if all of your tweets follow a central theme. For example, if you're looking to market yourself deeper into the music industry, keep your tweets centrally focused on music, artists, and so on, rather than jump from music to puppies to politics. People who are into music and the music industry will be more likely to follow individuals who keep to a consistent topic, rather than tweeting randomly on unrelated subjects.

38: Interact with Others

It may seem strange to respond to someone that you don't know—almost like sitting in a restaurant and overhearing a conversation at the next table and deciding to just jump in and give your two cents worth. But Twitter is a public forum, and it's perfectly okay to respond to people you don't know. If someone tweets "Not sure if I should have ice cream tonight, or stick to my diet" there's nothing wrong in tweeting back a quick and friendly, "Oh, go for the ice cream—diets are never fun!" It could be the start of other conversations.

39: Don't Get Sucked into One of the "Get 1,000 Friends Daily" Services

You'll see this offer around on Twitter constantly: tweets that provide a link, and promise that they can get you hundreds of new followers every day for free. Yeah, right! They're all scams. At the best, they'll ask you to log in with your Twitter username and password, and end up trying to hijack your account. At the worst, they'll con you into a "premium plan" that will cost you money for services you'll never receive.

40: Use the Right Tools

Your Twitter experience (and success) can be vastly improved if you use the right third-party tools. As I'm writing this, I have my favorites that I feel would enhance anybody's Twitter experience, but these have changed in just the last month or so. New tools come out so often that any list I can provide you will be outdated before this book even hits the printer, much less the shelf. So to preserve any type of relevancy, I'm going to limit my recommendations to the three best tools you should use for getting more contacts through Twitter—the three that I believe will still be viable well into the future:

- **TweetDeck (tweetdeck.com):** A hands down necessity to really enjoy and meet people through Twitter. Where Twitter provides only a single column of tweets (from people you're following by default), TweetDeck provides a number of columns to let you simultaneously monitor people you follow, tweets that mention you, direct messages, and any other keyword or group you want to check out.

- **Friend or Follow (friendorfollow.com):** This site will show you everyone you are following who is not following you back. This way, if there are certain people in particular you want to connect with, you know where to concentrate some additional efforts.

- **Twellow (twellow.com):** A yellow pages for Twitter, where you can put yourself into appropriate categories, and find relevant people to follow.

41: Don't Be Afraid to Send the Same Tweet Multiple Times

Some of the Twitter purists will tell you that it's bad form to send the same tweet multiple times. I disagree, and I'm not alone. The reality is that although you may have hundreds or even thousands of followers, it's possible that only a handful will see any given message that you tweet. First, people need to be on Twitter or some variation thereof at the time you send your tweet. As soon as you send it, it will fall one notch lower on the list when the next person sends a tweet, and so on until it falls out of people's line of sight altogether. So while I'm not advocating rapid-fire repeats of the same tweet, there's absolutely nothing wrong with sending the same tweet three of four times throughout the day to increase the likelihood that you'll reach a different audience each time.

42: Re-Tweet What Other People Write

One of the things that people tend to appreciate the most on Twitter is when people re-tweet them. Basically, that means taking their tweet and passing it on to your own network of followers. For example, let's say that I notice that @dbreakenridge (Deirdre Breakendridge, my business partner and public relations guru), sends out the following tweet:

Getting ready to host a PR student discussion at 3pm EST at #PRChat – please join!

I would send this to my own community of followers by re-tweeting it:

RT @dbreakenridge: Getting ready to host a PR student discussion at 3pm EST at #PRChat – please join!

The 'RT @dbreakenridge' that precedes the message means I am re-tweeting something that @dbreakenridge originally sent. By using her Twitter handle, she'll be notified that I've passed her tweet along.

So what does passing along someone else's message have to do with marketing yourself? Well, re-tweeting can bring along a number of benefits:

- It makes you more attractive for others to follow, as you'll seem to be less self-serving.
- Your own network of followers will appreciate receiving good information.
- The people you re-tweet will typically repay the effort by re-tweeting one or more of your messages.

If you use TweetDeck (see "Use the Right Tools" in this section), then re-tweeting is very easy and won't take more than a second.

43: Hold Twitter Chat Sessions

Assuming you have some credentials behind you—you've written a book, have achieved some degree of success in your industry, or something else—consider holding a Twitter-chat where students or professionals in your industry can ask you questions on specific topics. Simply start a group using a # tag, and get the word out through your network. Okay, maybe "simply" isn't the right word… it can be a challenge to get people to attend. But if you have accomplished something unique enough that people will believe they can learn from you, holding a question and answer chat session is a great way to get noticed and pick up a lot of followers.

44: Put Tweets into Relevant Groups for Other People to See and Find You

No matter what you're interested in, chances are there are keywords and groups you can view to gather more information and meet other like-minded people. For example (this is one of those tips I find it easiest to explain through my own experience), I mostly write, teach, and learn about marketing. So I keep an eye on any tweet people send that includes keywords like "marketing," "branding," and "advertising." When I see interesting people sending tweets with these words, I'll usually choose to follow them so I can keep a closer eye on what they're saying. At the same time, I want to make sure that other people in the marketing field can see what I'm writing. To do that, I try to make sure that I use the appropriate keywords in my tweets, and in instances where that just doesn't work, I tack it on at the end by using a # symbol. For example, the following tweet:

Currently writing my new book on marketing yourself.

will automatically show up when people search for the term "marketing" because I've used that word directly in my tweet. Not true of this tweet:

Currently writing my new book "101 Ways to Successfully Market Yourself."

This wouldn't show up in a search for marketing, because that word isn't used in the tweet. To make sure it shows up without having to change my sentence, I simply include a # term at the end:

Currently writing my new book "101 Ways to Successfully Market Yourself." #marketing

The # and keyword helps place my tweet in relevant searches without forcing me to include the word in my sentence.

Add # and keywords as often as possible (and only where relevant), to get you and your tweet seen by more people who may then be interested in following you.

45: Send Links

Very often, people will send links in their tweets, giving followers access to articles you find interesting (and that you believe others would find interesting, as well). This is a good way to contribute to the Twitter universe and be more attractive to potential followers.

When you tweet a link, make sure to first run it through a URL shortening service first. My personal recommendation is http://bit.ly because not only does it shorten your URL, but it allows you to instantly track how many times it has been clicked.

Facebook

46: Understand the Basic Concept

Originally created as a place for college students to network and connect with each other, Facebook has dethroned MySpace as the premier social network where people of all ages go to connect. A user-friendly, casual site, Facebook is primarily setup as a place for friends to connect, share pictures, play games, upload links, and otherwise stay in touch with each other. However, while it may be more of a "friendly" site, there is plenty of marketing, networking, and business to be done there.

47: Start Making Connections with People You Know

As with any other networking effort, on- or offline, your best place to start on Facebook is with the people you already know. Facebook will help you get connected with people from your e-mail address book and other sources, while a search feature can help you find individuals you may know and link up with.

48: Look Through Your Friends' Friends

Visit your friends' profile pages and look through the list of people they're friends with. Chances are, you'll recognize some of them and be able to make a new (or renew an old) connection.

49: Take Advantage of Facebook's Suggestion Feature

Based on your network and profile information that you've added, Facebook will regularly suggest new people it thinks you should connect with. Look through all of these suggestions, and add them to your network.

50: Don't Get Thrown Off by the Word "Friend"

I don't know how many times people have asked me, "Why is this person trying to be my friend? I don't even know her." Facebook's use of the word "friend" seems to trip up a lot of people. Don't read too deeply into it. While Facebook is used by many for casual connections rather than professional ones, there's room there for everyone. 'Friends' can literally mean people you're friends with, but it can also refer to acquaintances, associates, or people you don't know at all but would like to get to know better (for personal or professional reasons).

51: Join Facebook Groups and Fan Pages, or Start Your Own

Check out some of the user-initiated groups on Facebook by doing a search based on keywords associated with your particular interests, or by checking out some of the groups your Facebook friends are involved with. Sometimes these groups are fairly active, and group members get involved; other times the groups end up being fairly stagnant without a lot going on. It depends on the administrator, subject matter, and members. But either way, joining different groups will give you access to other members that you'll want to connect with. If the group is active, make sure to get in on the action and make yourself visible.

If there isn't an adequate group that covers your needs, or you just want to take a bit of initiative, you can start your own group, which will give you immediate access to new contacts who wish to join.

52: Make Connections from Groups You Join

Reach out to other people in groups that you join on Facebook and ask to make a friend connection. All it really takes is a short note, such as:

Hi! I noticed that we're both members of [NAME OF GROUP] and thought it might be a good idea to make a connection with you. Looking forward to finding out more about you.

The worst thing they can do is ignore you. But chances are, that won't happen. It's more likely you'll make a few new online friends and connections. Try and set a quota for yourself. For example, set a goal to reach out and extend a friend request to 10 new people each day.

53: "Like" and "Share" Other People's Links

When one of your connections posts a link on his page that you like, you have the option to share it (which means posting the link to your page as well), or to indicate that you "like" the link (which means that your name will appear on that person's page in association with the link he has posted). The more you do either of these, the more visible you'll become to people outside your immediate network.

54: Comment on People's Status Updates

Similar to using the "like" and "share" feature, Facebook allows you to post comments on the status updates (the few lines that people use to write what they're doing, thinking, or feeling) of people within your network. Comment on these when you can. It will make you more visible to the people in their networks as well.

LinkedIn

55: Understand the Basic Concept

LinkedIn is a social networking site for professionals, commonly used by people looking to find new employment or make business connections. Less intrusive than Facebook or Twitter, you'll have to work a little harder to meet people on LinkedIn, but the quality of connections is worth the effort.

56: Complete Your Profile as Thoroughly as Possible

While LinkedIn is a great site for networking, it can be a bit time-consuming to get started with—more so than many other networks. It's understandable, because after all, LinkedIn is for business networking, so filling out your profile is like filling out your resume: it takes awhile and it's not at all interesting. It'll seem even longer because you'll be anxious to get started and make some new connections. But don't rush through it. LinkedIn is one of the best ways to market yourself online, and your profile here really makes a difference. Fill it out as completely as possible before you start to make connections, including your current and past employers, schools attended, and special qualifications. LinkedIn will let you know how much of your profile you still have left to complete, and what steps you need to take to complete it, so you have no excuses for not doing it.

57: Start Connecting with People You Know (or May at Least Be Associated With)

In the next section on networking offline, I'll discuss beginning your self-marketing campaign adventures with people from your past. It's a good place to start on LinkedIn as well. LinkedIn enables you to search for contacts from previous employers and schools you've attended (colleges and universities, but not high school, unfortunately).

Similarly, LinkedIn enables you to connect with people you already have in your e-mail address book, which can also help get the ball rolling.

58: Look Through Your Connections' Connections

They say that there are six degrees of separation among every human being (and of course, Kevin Bacon). Well, start with the second degree—that alone will keep you busy enough. If you have 10 initial connections, and they each have 10 connections, that's 100 profiles to check out. There's a good chance you may even know some of those people.

Send requests to connect to anyone you may already know, as well as to people you'd like to associate with.

59: Don't Be Afraid To Ask for a Recommendation

LinkedIn allows people to write recommendations for each other, which can be meaningful to people interested in possibly working with you. But while it would be great for people to recommend you on their own accord, it's not often that people go out of their way to do so without being prompted. Don't be afraid to ask someone you know and trust to write you a recommendation. If she admires you and believes in your capabilities, then she'll be happy to help you out.

60: Join Groups and Take Part in Conversation

LinkedIn is home to many different member-initiated groups covering all sorts of topics. Doing a quick search for your area of interest will likely turn up any number of groups you can join. Do so. Each group is made up of other LinkedIn members that you can connect with, engaging in various conversations. Start your own or jump into an existing one. Either way, this is the heart of LinkedIn and one its best resources for meeting new people and marketing yourself, so don't sit on the sidelines—get involved.

Blogging and Other Online Efforts

61: Start Your Own Blog

For those not totally familiar with the term, a blog (shortened form of "we**b log**") is simply an online journal where you can record your thoughts on various topics that the public can read, share, and comment on. Having your own blog allows you to control the topic of conversation while giving you an outlet for writing your thoughts and letting potential contacts see what you know and what you're about. Use Twitter and other mechanisms to alert others about each new post you make to your blog.

While there are any number of ways to start your own blog, I'd strongly suggest looking into WordPress.com. WordPress is one of the best resources for maintaining your own blog presence—free, quick to set-up, and easy to create and update without needing to know a lot of code.

62: Update Your Blog Consistently

Like tweeting, going to networking events, or other forms of marketing, blogging can't be random, haphazard, or disorganized. To build an audience and keep people coming back, you're going to need to generate new content on a regular basis. Whether it's once a week, once every two weeks, or once a month (once a week is better), stay consistent and stick with it.

63: Get Your Name in a URL

While this is an especially important point if you have your own blog, make sure you secure the rights to your name as a URL. For example, I own both jaymiletsky.com (where my personal blog resides), and jasonmiletsky.com. Your name as a URL will be good marketing for any online activity that you engage in (starting a blog, for example), plus it is a good defensive measure. As you get yourself more out there, and more people know who you are, there's always the danger of someone else trying to cash in on your name by securing its URL.

64: Carefully Craft Your Signature (for Blog Comments and E-Mail)

Don't underestimate the importance of your digital signature. Along with your name, your digital signature can include your occupation, information on ways people can contact you, and other information that you'd like people to know. For example, my own digital signature looks like this:

Jay Miletsky

CEO, PFS Marketwyse

Author of Perspectives on Marketing and Perspectives on Branding

Web: http://www.jaymiletsky.com

Phone: 973.812.8883

Twitter: http://twitter.com/jaymiletsky

These signatures should be used everywhere you leave your name, including e-mails and comments on other people's blogs (discussed later in this section).

65: Say It on Online Radio

Online radio is quickly gaining in popularity. BlogTalkRadio and others have given aspiring talk show hosts the ability to easily (and without cost) have their own show on any topic they'd like. Chances are there are plenty of shows in your area of interest. Many of these are pretty informal, don't require any travel (you can phone in your interview from your home or office), and can draw a decent audience. Listen to some of the shows out there and shoot an e-mail asking to be interviewed (make sure you actually have something interesting to say, first!). Better yet, if you have the time and the drive to stick with it, start your own online radio show. It's easy, fun, you'll attract an audience, and you can endear yourself to desirable contacts by offering to interview them on your show.

66: Use the Power of Video

Most new computers come with built-in video cameras and basic, easy-to-use video capturing capabilities. For the computers that don't have cameras built in, external cameras are pretty inexpensive and simple to set-up. Consider putting your thoughts into a video blog posted to your own blog site and/or YouTube. Video helps people relate to you better, hear inflection in your voice, makes you more recognizable, and increases the likelihood that people will hear what you have to say (statistics show that more web users will spend more time watching a video than they will reading an article).

67: People Love Lists

Attract more people to your blog by creating lists. "Top 10 Fastest Ways to Lose Weight," "5 Best Travel Destinations on a Budget," "101 Ways to Successfully Market Yourself." Maybe it's because the list format piques our curiosity, or maybe it's because we know a list is easy and quick to read. Whatever the reason, if you want to attract an audience and get people to read what you have to say, put it in a list.

68: Comment on Other People's Blogs

Your own blog isn't the only place you can make your voice heard and your name visible. Find other people's blogs—particularly those that are well-read and within your scope of interest, and leave comments stating your own opinions on the topic at hand. Regardless of whether you agree or disagree, it's a good way of making your voice heard by a lot of other people and getting involved in the conversation. Make sure you use a signature (as discussed earlier in this section) that lets all other blog readers know who you are and how they can contact you.

69: Broadcast What You Write

Although I've divided the online section of the book into separate, smaller parts, look for opportunities to put them all together in order to attract more attention. For example, each time you write a blog post of your own, or leave a comment on someone else's blog, get the URL for the post and shorten it (through bit.ly or some other shortening service), and broadcast it out on Twitter a few times throughout the day, use it in a conversation on LinkedIn, post it in relevant Facebook groups you belong to and leave it as a link on your Facebook wall. Leveraging each of these and finding ways to use them together will make all of your online efforts to market yourself more effective.

70: Look into Hosting a Free Webinar

Basically, Webinars are online seminars. If you can come up with a topic that's interesting enough, look into hosting one of your own. There are any number of resources online that will help you facilitate your Webinar. Most cost some money, but they're not all that expensive, and will allow you to control the show, upload your own PowerPoint deck or other file, hold public or private discussions with attendees, and collect all attendee contact information. Webinars give you a chance to be the star of the show, and as such, if attendees like what they're hearing, you'll raise your profile and become someone that others actively want to connect with.

Make your presentation available to attendees after you're finished, with your name and contact information clearly visible so people can connect with you later.

Increase awareness of your Webinar by sending e-mails to all your connections and posting a link to the online registration on Facebook, Twitter, LinkedIn, and any other network you're a part of. You may also want to consider presenting your Webinar in conjunction with a larger organization, such as an active Chamber of Commerce, to get their help in driving traffic as well.

71: E-Mail Marketing Can Be Powerful

Now, the official laws about e-mailing and the advice I'm about to give you may be just slightly different, so if you end up being carted away to prison or hit with a huge fine, don't blame me.

That being said, I am *not* condoning spam. Not at all. I get more junk mail in my spam folder than I like to think about. I can't tell you how many times I've won some European lottery that I never entered, and how much money I've apparently inherited from wealthy Nigerians over the years. But in terms of legitimate marketing efforts, e-mail marketing is a method you should actively take advantage of, especially to alert people to new blog posts you've written, Webinars, or speaking engagements you may be featured in, or any other legitimate reason to keep your name in front of people.

With e-mail marketing you can:

- Send e-mails that look like your website, using HTML code for unique layout and design.
- Include links to your site, blog, Twitter account, and more.
- Get your message in front of new, existing, and potential contacts immediately and without a very high cost.
- Track how many people opened your e-mail, when, and who clicked a link, and which links they clicked.

The question of legality comes in the acquisition of the e-mails that you send, and whether or not you're allowed to send them promotional-based e-mails. I'm not a lawyer, so I'm not going to quote on what you can or can't do—that's something you should check out for yourself before doing anything with e-mail marketing. Personally, I've built my e-mail marketing lists from a collection of all contacts I've made. I also gather the e-mail address of anyone I'm on a CC list with, and at times have visited websites for various organizations, such as Chambers of Commerce, and copied and pasted e-mail addresses for their members (if they're posted online).

If you engage in e-mail marketing, don't make a pest of yourself. Limit contact to no more than once per week. That's usually enough to keep yourself recognizable without becoming too much of a nuisance.

72: Post Your Skills on Craigslist

Craigslist.com is the leading online source for classified ads, offering uncountable numbers of posts in a wide variety of categories and geographic locations. And the best part is that with some very few exceptions, posting an ad on Craigslist is free. Find the category that most applies to your personal goals, and continue posting ads to draw attention.

73: Look for Online Lists

Earlier, I mentioned that people love lists. Not only do they like reading them, but they like writing them as well. With a little bit of effort you can find tons of lists that will make it easy to track down new resources for connecting with people. Go to Google and do a search for "Best blogs in [INSERT YOUR AREA OF EXPERTISE]," "Best people to follow on Twitter in [INSERT YOUR AREA OF INTEREST]," "Best Link-In groups in [INSERT YOUR AREA OF INTEREST]," and similar searches. While not every list will be spot on, more often than not most of them will give you some great links to sites, groups, people, and resources that you should take the time to get involved with.

PART III

THERE'S LIFE OFFLINE—
GET OUT AND MEET
REAL PEOPLE

There's no question that social media has changed the way we market ourselves, and opened new opportunities for building a following. But with all the hype of online networking, it's easy to think that the best or only way of successfully promoting yourself is to never turn your back on the laptop. Well, I'm sorry to have to break it to you, but at some point you're going to need to pry your backside off the couch and get out into the real world, because not only is meeting people face to face still relevant, it's necessary.

74: Know What You're About and Be Able to Explain It Easily

I detest the term "elevator speech," because it's just so overused, but for lack of a better term I'll stick with it. For anyone not familiar with the term, an elevator speech is an explanation or description of yourself that can be given quickly—in about the time it takes to ride an elevator. The fact is, not a lot of people are going to hang around to listen to you recite a full thesis. Everyone is busy, everyone has his or her own agenda—people you connect with don't have all day to get to know you.

Know what you do, what you can offer people, and what you're looking for, and figure out how to express all of it in less than 30 seconds. Believe it or not, it actually takes a bit of practice, so while you don't want to sound like a robot, it never hurts to rehearse your elevator speech a bit before you start making connections. Remember that 50% of the term "marketing yourself" is "marketing" so do exactly that, and spin your speech so that you appear intriguing, interesting, and engaging.

75: Start with People with Whom You've Lost Touch

At the beginning of the marketing-yourself process, it's easy to feel overwhelmed and not know where to start. It's easy to forget how many people you already know, and how many connections you've already made in your lifetime.

Talk to your friends and family. Let them know what you're trying to do and accomplish. Ask them if they know anybody that they can introduce you to or put you in contact with. Be specific in explaining the type of people you want to meet because once your friends and family make a connection for you, whether it's to the right person or not, you're going to be obligated to at least meet and speak with that person. Reduce the potential wasted time by explaining exactly who you want to get to know.

After your friends and family, reach into your past. Whatever happened to the friends and acquaintances you made in high school, summer camp, college, sports teams, summer jobs, or around the neighborhood? You never know what some of them might be up to these days, and the kinds of connections you can make by getting back in touch with people you already know.

76: Shop Around for the Best Networking Events, and Frequent Them Often

While it's always nice to meet random contacts in unexpected places, you need to get out and hit the networking events. (I once chatted with a woman standing behind me in line at a Sbarros pizza place. Turned out she was the Director of Communications for a small medical device company, and later, a new client!) Most of these networking events can actually be a lot of fun—you mingle, have a drink or two—but they can also be time consuming and potentially expensive (some require a fee to get in, plus there's parking, tolls, bar tabs, and so on). Clearly, you can't go to every one that comes your way, so be selective:

- Pick events that will be more lively and social.

- Events held in bars, especially in a city, tend to draw more people.

- If the event has a decent speaker, that also could be a draw for a larger crowd.

- Choose events based on your goals for marketing yourself. For example, if you're looking to increase sales, you want to go to networking events where you can meet potential clients, not talk to people from your own industry. On the other hand, if you're looking for a new job, people within your industry are exactly who you want to hang out with.

You can usually find networking events simply by checking out Google, MeetUp.com, or by asking other people in and around your industry which events they usually go to.

77: Work the Trade Shows

There's no question that trade shows' traffic and viability have been on the wane since the explosion of the Web has given people greater access to information. But besides being informative and sometimes fun, trade shows bring together buyers and sellers with like-minded interests that are there for the purposes of meeting other people.

78: Volunteer to Lead or Be on a Committee

What??? I must be kidding—you have enough to do as it is. I can't possibly be suggesting that you take on more work, and do it for *free*! Well, as hard as it might be to swallow, volunteering can be one of the best ways there is to meet like-minded people. Through meetings and deadlines, it forces people to get together and stay in touch, and can put you in front of a large number of group members in a leadership role.

However, before you go raising your hand to head up the entertainment committee for some organization, keep in mind the following:

- Make sure the group has a good number of members that you would actually benefit from getting connected with.

- Make sure you volunteer for a committee that you actually understand, that you'll enjoy, and that you actually have some knowledge about.

- Make sure the group is made up of people who are committed to actually doing some work, and it won't end up being a long series of missed meetings and cancellations.

- Make sure you yourself are committed to seeing it through— while volunteering for an organization can help you meet people, it can similarly damage your reputation if you never show up, fail to meet your commitments, and never follow through with anything.

79: Become a Regular

It's easier to meet people once you recognize each other, so become a regular in various places. For example, organizers of good networking events will usually try to keep them going on a regular basis, like once each month. Make a habit of going to as many of these as possible so people recognize your face over time.

80: Create a Memorable Business Card, and Remember to Bring Plenty with You

It's amazing how much power a 3-inch piece of paper can wield, but there's no denying that business cards say a lot more about you than the information printed on them. A well designed card can be eye-catching, memorable, and tell your contacts about your style, personality, and professionalism. Some of the ways that people have created stand-out cards have been the use of brighter, bolder colors, rounded corners, die cuts, heavier paper, non-typical sizes, and, of course, more artistic designs.

In *American Psycho*, not only did the superficial '80s era Wall Street types compete with one another for the coveted honor of having the most perfect business card, but the lead character actually offed his rival for outdoing him. (If you haven't read the book or seen this movie, I suggest you search "American Psycho business card" to watch it on YouTube. The subtle, dark humor is outstanding.) Never underestimate the importance of the perfect business card!

In terms of information, look beyond the typical standards of name, title, address, office phone, and e-mail. Consider adding your cell phone number and Twitter handle, and Linked-In URL as well.

And finally, not to belabor the business card conversation, but make sure you always have some on you, especially when you'll be in networking situations. You'll look very disorganized and unprofessional if you meet people and don't have a card, and nobody believes the lame "they're still at the printers" excuse.

81: Don't Rely on Your Memory

No matter how great you think your memory is, don't count on it. As you begin to market yourself, you'll start meeting a *lot* of people, and they'll quickly start to blend into one another. The one thing you don't want is to meet somebody, look at his business card a few days later, and not be able to remember who he was or what you talked about. Every time that happens, it's pretty much a wasted contact. Best thing to do: for each new contact, jot a couple of notes down on the back of the person's business card to help jog your memory later. These notes could be about your conversation, what the person wore, a physical attribute that really stood out—anything that will help you recall the person after the fact.

82: Seek Out Public Speaking Opportunities

Want to meet a lot of people all at once? Be a featured speaker in a room full of people who are listening. Speakers command attention, and are points of focus for attendees, many of whom will want to talk to you afterward and get to know you better.

Before seeking out speaking opportunities, you need to determine the specific subjects you want to speak about—the topics that you know the best and speak about most eloquently. Once you have the topics in hand, reach out to organizers of seminars, networking events, chambers of commerce, universities, industry organizations, and other outlets to let them know you're available, willing to speak, and can offer their audience unique information.

83: Use a Crutch If It Helps

One of the concerns people often have when marketing themselves is that they don't know what to do with their hands when they're talking to people, especially in social situations such as networking events. Do you fold your arms? Put your hands in your pockets? The easiest solution is just to hold something, like a drink. Whether or not you use the object you're holding doesn't matter—the mere act of holding something can give you the little extra security you need to converse comfortably.

84: Don't Get Sucked into Talking to Any One Person for Too Long

While it's true that quality is always better than quantity, you're going to want to meet a good number of people anytime you're in a social situation. Don't get trapped by any one person who feels the need to drone on and on about their life, job, recent surgery, daughter's upcoming graduation, blah, blah, blah, and keep you from meeting other people. It can be very frustrating.

I remember one time in particular that I went to a networking event, hoping to expand my connections and meet a few new potential clients. I ended up chatting with a guy who had just recently gotten laid off, and was looking for work. Nice guy, and I felt for him, and I was happy to stay in touch—maybe I could pass his resume on to someone and help him, or maybe one day he'd have a job and be in a position to give me some work—but 15 minutes later I was feeling considerable angst that I was still standing there listening to his plight. I wanted to meet more people!

The hard part in situations like this is excusing yourself without being obvious or impolite. Some of the methods I've found for doing this successfully include:

- Finishing my drink and excusing myself to get another one (don't make the mistake of offering to get this individual a drink or you'll be bound to return and pick up the conversation where it left off).

- Explaining that I'm waiting for a friend to arrive, and need to run out and see if he has arrived or call to see if he's on his way.

- Looking at my watch and explaining that I need to run out and call a client or spouse.

- And, of course, the easiest excuse of all—needing to use the restroom. (Use this excuse sparingly, especially if you're speaking with someone of the same gender— the last thing you need is to have a conversation follow you into the restroom.)

85: Buy the First Round... or Any Round

Buying a round of drinks for people when you're out at a networking event makes them feel appreciative and indebted, and makes you look like a good guy. Not buying one, especially when others are buying rounds, makes you look cheap. You do the math.

86: Be Less Drunk than Everyone Else in the Room

Just a simple little social rule, when it comes to marketing yourself, you need to make a good impression. Watch how much you drink and don't lose control of yourself.

87: Don't Go It Alone

There will be plenty of times that you'll need to fly solo when marketing yourself, especially in instances where you find yourself among people and can make quick one-on-one connections. However, if you are planning to go to a social outing, like a seminar, tradeshow or networking event, try to go with someone else rather than go it alone. There's strength in numbers, and you can introduce each other to new people you both meet, thereby doubling the number of connections you'll make. It's also easier to bring people into a conversation that you're having with the person you came with, and it'll give you someone to talk to when you need a break from networking, rather than just standing awkwardly in a corner all alone.

88: Take Advantage of a Captive Audience

Don't take this the wrong way. I'm not advocating that you be smothering, but there will be times when you find yourself with a captive audience, and when you do, you should take advantage of the opportunity. There are probably more of these opportunities than you realize:

- Sitting next to someone on a plane, train, or bus.
- Standing with someone else in a long elevator.
- Standing in a long line (people behind and in front of you are easy targets for conversations).
- Sitting next to someone at a Starbucks or other café.
- Sitting next to someone at a concert, musical, or play (before the show starts).

The list goes on. Keep your eyes open for these and similar opportunities and do what you can to make a connection. You never know who you're going to meet!

89: Join a Club or Other Social Group

Have a hobby? You can enjoy it and meet new people at the same time. Look around the Web, your local paper, or just ask around. Chances are you'll find a group you can join for just about anything you enjoy from softball, volleyball, and tennis, to photography, baking, and bike riding. Take an active role in one or more of these groups, or even volunteer to do some community service. You'll not only have fun, but you'll meet a lot of great connections, too.

90: Host a Social Party

Everyone likes a party, and few people need a reason to go to one. So host one yourself. Tell the people you invite to bring a friend or two of their own, and you'll find yourself hosting a party packed with new people for you to meet.

91: Host or Organize an Event

Similar to hosting a party, consider hosting or joining an event like a book club or friendly poker game. These types of low-key social events give everyone an opportunity to talk leisurely with a built-in commonality from which to start a conversation.

92: Marketing Yourself Doesn't Stop During Vacation

Not only does marketing yourself not stop during a vacation, it can actually improve during that time. Vacations are a great place to meet people and strike up conversations. Everyone is more relaxed on vacation, their guard is down, and there are usually plenty of opportunities to meet new people: hotel pools or Jacuzzi's, concierge lounges, guided tours, local bars, restaurants and clubs, the airport to and from your destination. Regardless of where you go, don't put your marketing yourself campaign on hold—instead, turn it up a notch.

93: Check Out Your College's Alumni Association

If you went to college, get involved with the alumni association. Most schools will run events, such as seminars, dinners, or continued learning for graduated students, organized by industry and by geography. Even if you've stayed in touch with all your college friends, networking through your alumni association is a good place to make new connections. There's usually a sense of loyalty and camaraderie among people who have gone to the same school, so connections made through alumni functions could be particularly strong. Same goes for fraternities and sororities, school clubs, and sports teams.

94: Remember Names

I love it when people forget someone's name about a minute after being introduced, and then laugh it off by saying, "Oh, I've always been terrible with names!" Isn't that just so cute and forgivable? No, actually it is rude and off-putting. It's a name, not the Declaration of Independence, for crying out loud. Repeat the name after you first hear it, come up with a word that rhymes with it or something you can associate with it—whatever it takes to remember the person's name, do it.

95: Look for Easy Conversation Starters

Earlier in this book, I mentioned that people won't bite if you simply put your hand out and introduce yourself. But I know that for many people, no matter what assurances I give, it is an act that's easier said than done. So, to make it a bit easier, look for opportunities to start conversations that make an approach more natural:

- Ask to borrow a pen to jot a quick note.
- If you see someone drop something, make the effort to pick it up for them. Similarly, if you see someone struggling to carry something or hold a door open while his hands are full, offer to help.
- Ask for easy help (directions to a specific place, recommendations for a good restaurant in the area, and so on).
- Comment or ask about something the other person has out in the open. For example, maybe she's working on a laptop or holding a certain cell phone—ask how she likes that model, and whether she would recommend you getting one.

96: Don't Make Uncomfortable Jokes or Comments

While it's good to be humble, putting yourself down—even jokingly—can make people uncomfortable. This is especially true when you first meet or are getting to know someone new. For example, when someone comments that food is good, responding with "Yeah, too good. I already have to lose 10 pounds!" makes the other person uncomfortable. The other person may not be sure whether to laugh along with you, or feel forced to say, "No, you don't have to lose any weight. You look great." Either way, it makes conversations awkward and uneasy, and neither is a good launching pad for establishing a new connection.

97: Use Your Kids

Kids usually have no problem meeting other kids and making friends. Those connections create an easy way to get to know their friends' parents. Go to their school functions and sporting events where many of the other parents gather. Having your kids in common is an easy way to start new conversations and meet new people.

98: Wait Tables

Waiting tables is tough work, there's no doubt about it. I've done it and hated every minute of it. But it puts you in front of a lot of people who expect to converse with you. This is especially helpful for students who are still in school or have recently graduated, as customers are often interested in what their future plans are. Don't be afraid to leave your business cards with customers. Many of my own early marketing customers were people who I met while waiting on them.

99: Still Young? Play the Cute, Ambitious Kid Card

Ah, if I had only realized how much easier marketing myself was when I was young(er). Everybody wants to help the cute, motivated, hard-working kid make something of himself. If you're still in your twenties, play up the age card, and allow people who are older than you to think they're playing a big role in your development. Older, established people always want to feel like they've really helped the up-and-coming kid.

100: Get a Puppy (or a Babysitting Job)

I am not a dog person. At least, I never was one growing up, so I'm as surprised as anybody that I'm adding this point to the overall list. But I recently began dating a woman with a dog, and over the last few months, I've noticed something amazing: it's literally impossible to take the dog for a walk without meeting someone new. If it's a longer walk through a populated area, the cumulative amount of time spent on conversations that take place will usually last longer than the actual time spent walking. Apparently, dog people can't see a dog without stopping and chatting. First about the dog, then about the neighborhood, and before you know it, you've made a new connection. Crazy, but true. And if you can't get a puppy, find someone with a baby and borrow it every now and then—the same basic rule applies with babies, especially ones in cute clothes.

101: Make Follow-Up a Ritual

Making that initial connection is only half the battle. Connections won't do you much good if you forget about them soon after—or worse still, let them forget about you. Make sure you follow up with each new contact through a quick e-mail within 24 hours after making an initial connection, remind the new contact of who you are, how you met, what you talked about, and, if in cases where you think a connection may be of use to you, suggest times and reasons to get together again.

Appendix A

Best Twitter Tools

Twitter is one of the absolute best ways to get people to notice you. Will it always be as powerful as it is now? That's hard to say. In many ways, social media is still in its infancy, and as a bunch of bewildered execs over at MySpace will attest, there's no telling when the next big thing will come along and dethrone the reigning king. But for the foreseeable future, Twitter is going to be a formidable player to use to market yourself. To help you get the most of it, I've provided a list of 30 great Twitter tools. Please keep in mind that nobody needs to use *all* of these tools. While I personally use many of them, I haven't tried them all—some are recommendations from friends and people I follow on Twitter. So if any of the sites below ends up being a bad egg…don't blame me! Find the right fit for you and your needs and goals to successfully market yourself.

TweetDeck
(tweetdeck.com)

A hands down necessity to really enjoy and meet people through Twitter. Where Twitter provides only a single column of Tweets (from people you're following, by default), TweetDeck provides a number of columns to let you simultaneously monitor people you follow, tweets that mention you, direct messages, and any other keyword or group you want to check out. You'll have to download it and install it on your system.

TwitPic
(twitpic.com)

The best way to share pictures through Twitter. Particularly helpful if you're in an industry that requires you to have and show some sort of a portfolio.

Friend or Follow
(friendorfollow.com)

This site will show you everyone you are following who is not following you back. This is especially helpful if there are certain people in particular you want to connect with. It will help you identify where to concentrate some additional effort in your marketing campaign.

Twellow
(twellow.com)

A Yellow Pages for Twitter, where you can put yourself into appropriate categories, and find relevant people to follow.

Mr. Tweet
(mrtweet.com)

One of the only reputable online sources that will help make connections for you (most of the others are sketchy at best, and outright cons at the worst). Mr. Tweet will make recommendations for you, allow you to check out who is following you that you may not yet be following, and provide important stats to gauge your Twitter usage.

WeFollow
(wefollow.com)

Wonderful resource for finding new people to follow, and letting new people find you based on keywords and categories.

Just Tweet It
(justtweetit.com)
A very convenient way to interact with other people and let them find you based on similar interests.

Who Should I Follow
(whoshouldifollow.com)
Simply enter your Twitter name into this site, and based upon your info and tweets, Who Should I Follow will make relevant recommendations for people you should check out. Remember, as you follow more people, more people will follow you back.

Nearby Tweets
(nearbytweets.com)
An awesome tool for those who want to market themselves closer to home. Simply enter in a geographical location, enter a keyword that you're interested in, and Nearby Tweets shows you all of the people within a designated radius that fit the description. This is one of my favorite tools.

Twitterholic
(twitterholic.com)
This is another one of my favorite tools. Twitterholic is a great resource for checking your relative ranking and a graph of your followers over time.

TwitterFriends
(twitter-friends.com)
A great tracking and graphic tool that will pretty much give you any info you need in terms of your Twitter account and conversations—maybe too much because you easily can lose yourself in this site.

Twitbuttons
(twitbuttons.com)

Enables you to copy the code for your favorite "Follow Me" icons and paste it into your Web page or blog to allow visitors to easily find and follow you on Twitter.

Twitzu
(twitzu.com)

Tons of great resources here for marketing with Twitter. Like a big tool box full of... a lot of different tools.

Timer
(twitter.com/timer)

Follow Timer on Twitter and send them a message about when you need to be reminded of something (say, to go to a meeting in three hours). Timer will send you a direct message at the requested time to remind you. Kind of like a hotel wake-up call, but without the annoyingly loud phone interrupting you right in the middle of a dream.

Search Twitter
(search.twitter.com)

Use this site to keep track of anything at all—including anytime your name comes up in people's Twitter conversations, and to see which topics are currently the most popular.

SocialOomph
(socialoomph.com)

If you're too busy to sit and watch TweetDeck all day long, then this tool will help. SocialOomph allows you to schedule your Tweets to be sent later, so you'll be on the grid and still picking up new followers even when you're nowhere near a computer.

Twuffer

(twuffer.com)

Another tool that allows you to schedule your tweets in advance.

TweetBeep

(tweetbeep.com)

Want to know when someone mentions you in their tweet without having to look it up yourself? Sign up for TweetBeep, and you'll be alerted through e-mail. Handy to have so you know when and to whom to respond and reach out to.

TweetShrink

(tweetshrink.com)

Twitter's 140 character limit can be somewhat... well, limiting. And tough to send longer tweets. TweetShrink will help you shorten your tweets and lose unnecessary characters.

Tweet for iPhone

(tweetforiphone.com)

You don't plan on social networking without an iPhone, do you? Well, actually, I don't have an iPhone myself. Yet! But for those iPhone owners out there, this is apparently the best there is for using Twitter from your mobile device.

TwitterBerry

(orangatame.com/products/twitterberry)

For those with a Blackberry instead of an iPhone, this is your Twitter app.

Twitter Counter
(twittercounter.com)

This tool allows you to show how many Twitter followers you have on your site or blog. It's a great way for integrating different media to build awareness.

TweetStats and TwitGraph
(tweetstats.com) (twitgraph.com)

Both of these sites are somewhat ugly and rudimentary, but they do a good job of displaying your vital stats in graph format. These will help you see who you most actively correspond with and when.

Tweet Value
(tweetvalue.com)

This tool will show you how much your Twitter account is worth. Not really all that useful in practice, but it's kind of fun and interesting to track once your account starts accumulating value.

TwitterFeed
(twitterfeed.com)

Another great tool for integrating media, TwitterFeed will send your blog info to Twitter. Great tracking and stats info.

Twibs
(twibs.com/)

This site allows you to find, follow, and interact with businesses. If you're marketing your own company, look for the link that allows you to add your business to the list.

StrawPoll

(strawpollnow.com)

Easily create and review polls given to Twitter users to track opinions. Great for getting a pulse on people's feelings and knowing how best to approach certain topics, as well as give you a reason for interacting with people you don't know yet.

Twitter Friends Network Browser

(neuroproductions.be/twitter_friends_network_browser)

Very cool and useful way of checking out other people's network to see who you might be interested in following as well.

twtQpon

(twtqpon.com)

Have something to sell? Use this service to offer people on Twitter discount coupons for purchasing your product.

Twittertise

(twittertise.com)

This tool allows you to advertise on Twitter and track the success of branded communications with your customers. Gives you access to scheduling, URL tracking, and measurement.

"Who You Should Follow on Twitter" Lists

One of the hardest things about Twitter is finding good people to follow. As I've mentioned a few times throughout this book, the more people you follow, the more people will follow you, and then BAM! you've got yourself a network. But finding people to follow isn't all that hard—the trick is to find *relevant* people to follow. People who matter to your networking goal, and who you would genuinely want to interact with. To help find these people, some individuals keep running lists of the best people in certain categories for you to check out and follow. This appendix is a list of those lists.

To make things easier, you can also find this list along with active links, on my personal blog at jaymiletsky.com in the Resources section.

Top Marketing Book Authors

Yours truly is on this list—sorry, I just had to mention it!

http://www.systemicmarketing.com/top-marketing-book-authors-on-twitter/

Top CMOs

http://www.systemicmarketing.com/top-cmos-on-twitter/

Top Marketing Professors

http://www.systemicmarketing.com/top-marketing-professors-on-twitter/

100 PR People Worth Following
http://www.conversationagent.com/2009/09/100-pr-people-worth-following-on-twitter.html

Top Generally Interesting People
http://carsonified.com/blog/features/the-most-interesting-people-to-follow-on-twitter/

Top 100 Geeks
http://www.wired.com/geekdad/2009/05/100-geeks-you-should-be-following-on-twitter/

35 Web Analytics and Internet Marketing Experts
http://rich-page.com/web-analytics/35-web-analytics-internet-marketing-experts-you-should-be-following-on-twitter/

Vegans and Vegetarians
http://www.groovyvegetarian.com/2009/04/10/vegetarians-and-vegans-on-twitter/

200 Internet Marketing Gurus
http://www.marketingpilgrim.com/2008/01/internet-marketing-experts-twitter.html

100 Top People in HR
http://steveboese.squarespace.com/journal/2009/1/30/your-first-100-hr-twitter-follows.html

145 Top Lawyers
http://scoop.jdsupra.com/2008/09/articles/law-firm-marketing/145-lawyers-and-legal-professionals-to-follow-on-twitter/

30 Young Entrepreneurs

http://www.retireat21.com/blog/30-young-entrepreneurs-you-should-be-following-on-twitter/

101 Sports Blogs and Bloggers

http://hailmaryjane.com/101-sports-blogs-and-bloggers-you-should-be-following-on-twitter/

50 Users to Follow for Job Searching

http://www.onedayonejob.com/blog/50-twitter-users-to-follow-for-your-job-search/

125 People Personal Finance Junkies Should Follow

http://www.biblemoneymatters.com/2008/12/125-more-people-personal-finance-junkies-should-follow-on-twitter.html

Top 150 Marketing and Advertising People

http://www.twitterpower150.com/

80+ Environmental Organizations

http://planetsave.com/blog/2009/05/12/80-environmental-organizations-to-follow-on-twitter/

50 People for Job Seekers to Follow

http://www.resumebear.com/blog/index.php/2009/04/19/50-people-on-twitter-job-seekers-should-follow/

Top CEOs

http://images.businessweek.com/ss/09/05/0508_ceos_who_twitter/index.htm

Most Influential Female Designers

http://velvetant.net/blog/influential-female-designers/

Top 237 People to Follow That Will Follow You Back

http://socialnewswatch.com/top-twitter-users/

Another 1,001 People Who Will Follow You Back

http://www.sebastienpage.com/2009/03/23/1001-twitter-users-follow-back/

The Best List of Moms

http://www.sparkplugging.com/sparkplug-ceo/the-ultimate-list-of-moms-on-twitter/

40+ Winos

http://drinksareonme.net/2008/05/25/40-winos-to-follow-on-twitter/

85 Comedians

http://mashable.com/2009/05/26/twitter-comedians/

25 SEO Gurus

http://www.dailyseoblog.com/2009/01/25-seo-gurus-you-should-follow-on-twitter/

70 Non Fiction Authors

http://mashable.com/2009/05/22/twitter-nonfiction-authors/

638 Architects

http://www.justpractising.com/architects-twitter-league/

50 Product Managers

http://www.webproductblog.com/web-product-management/
50-product-managers-in-twitter-that-are-worth-a-follow/

The Ultimate List of Dads and Husbands

http://www.sparkplugging.com/the-man-page/the-ultimate-twit-list-
dads-and-husbands-on-twitter/

Top 1 Author of 101 Ways to Successfully Market Yourself

http://twitter.com/jaymiletsky

Appendix C

LinkedIn Groups

For professional networking, LinkedIn can be an amazing resource. But it takes more of an effort than just posting your resume information. To really take advantage of everything the site has to offer, you have to be actively involved, and a big part of that is joining LinkedIn groups and having your voice heard in various conversations.

As with any site that allows users to control content, there are going to be some groups that are better and more worth your time than others. The values to look for in a group are how many people play an active role, the overall quality of the conversations (are people really talking, as opposed to just selling), and how often new topics are started. To help you narrow down the best groups, I've provided a pretty comprehensive list in this appendix. The links for these groups are pretty long, so rather than print them here, I'd suggest either doing a search for each group from LinkedIn, or link to each directly from my blog at jaymiletsky.com.

For Entrepreneurs

OnStartups
One of the largest LinkedIn groups in this category with over 100,000 members, this is an active group that concentrates on the specific challenges faced by small business owners.

DFW Entrepreneur Network

You'll find some great conversations here from serious-minded entrepreneurs and some interesting people to connect with.

Start-Up Phase Forum

Living up to its name, this group actively provides a forum for entrepreneurs in the start-up phase to meet other business owners and potential clients, as well as resources for marketing, legal advice, and financial consulting.

For Marketers

EMarketing Association Network

A LinkedIn powerhouse, this group is closing in on 200,000 members, and may already surpass that by the time this book is in print. It's managed by the eMarketing Association—a prominent entity in the marketing world, holding numerous seminars, conferences, and events throughout the year. This LinkedIn group will keep you busy with plenty of quality discussions and provide access to some great new connections.

Marketing & PR Innovators

You'll find some excellent discussions going on in this group, which stays well focused on marketing and public relations issues. Members are very active and keep the conversations flowing.

Social Media Marketing

For those interested in making new connections and joining conversations based on social media marketing, social networking, and other online efforts, you'll want to check out this popular and active group.

For Job Seekers

CareerLink Network

This is a nice-sized group that caters to individuals looking for new careers or wanting to advance their current jobs. While you may find potential employers here to connect with, the real value is the advice and support the group and its members can give in your career endeavors.

JobAngels

A good group that connects people who are looking for jobs with people who can help them find jobs. This resource actively tries to create new, high quality connections for individuals shopping for new employment.

The Talent Buzz

This is a good group for making connections with HR managers, recruiters, and head hunters, many of whom take part in ongoing online discussions with job seekers and potential candidates. Conversations include marketing, HR topics, social media, and more.

For People Interested in Finance

Finance Club

Great resource for meeting and interacting with accountants, investors, bankers, venture capitalists, and other financial service professionals. Look here to engage in topical conversations and find potential sales and job leads.

Finance & Accounting Professionals

Everything and anything finance! You'll find financial people from all across the spectrum in this group, with plenty of opportunities to connect and interact.

Private Equity and Venture Capital Group

A little more focused than other groups in this category, members of this organization actively discuss investment opportunities and seek out alternative investment strategies. If you're looking for funding for a new business, this could be a good resource.

Freelancers and Consultants

Consultants Network

Whatever kind of consultant you are—business, finance, IT, marketing, programming, design, freelancer—with nearly 100,000 members this group will have something valuable for you. It's not only a resource for you to interact with and meet other consultants, but there are good opportunities to connect with potential customers as well.

Freelance Professionals

This group focuses a bit more on the tech and creative sector, with most members working as art directors, copywriters, graphic designers, programmers, Flash developers, etc. There are some great resources here and a chance to be noticed by your peers.

Designers Talk

This one is really focused—catering to over 10,000 graphic and web designers, brand developers, photographers, and the like. There's a chance you could get some work from people you meet in this group, but even more interesting are the opportunities for brainstorming new ideas and getting relevant feedback from like-minded individuals on your work.

Appendix D

Other Social Networks to Consider

Within the constraints of featuring only 101 tips in the main text, I had to be pretty careful about which tips I provided. The truth is that I could have gone on and on, reached 1,001 tips and still felt like I had more to write. One area in particular that I feel obligated to include is direction to other great social networks outside the "Big 3" (Facebook, Twitter, and LinkedIn) that I discussed. With literally thousands of quality networks online, there are more than enough opportunities to meet the right people and market yourself effectively. However, joining new sites, understanding what they each do, how they work, and building up a network can be exhausting—and a waste of time if you end up joining a network that won't really work for you. So to ease the pain, I've put together the following list of other networks in various categories that you might want to consider. You can find links to each in the Resources page of my blog at jaymiletsky.com.

For Job Hunters

The sites listed here are ones that allow you to engage, market yourself, and network—not sites that simply function as job boards.

Jobster
(jobster.com)

Jobster acts as both a social network and a job board. Post up your resume, add a video resume, tag your skills, provide links to your site, and search for jobs in your area of expertise that have been posted by employers with positions to fill. Better yet, connect with those employers and engage in an online dialog to learn more about each other and the potential position.

Ecadamy
(ecademy.com)

As of this writing, Ecademy doesn't have a job search feature, focusing instead on providing jobs through social networking. Set up your profile and let people know who you are and what you do. Then find the best on-site business networking groups for you and your area of expertise and let the magic happen. Chat publicly or privately with both other job seekers and potential employers.

MyWorkster
(myworkster.com)

A brilliant concept that creates career networking possibilities by joining job seekers with employers through their college connections. Earlier in this book I mentioned that people tend to be more willing to help other graduates of the schools they've attended, and this site puts that philosophy into practice.

For Generation Y (Millenials)

Gen Y grew up with social media technology. Where I ran home after school to pick up the phone and call my friends, Generation Y, otherwise known as the Millenials, ran home to jump on their instant messengers. Later, they didn't run home at all, chatting away instead on their mobile devices. Well, that generation is out of school and now in the working world, and there are plenty of networking sites that cater to their needs.

MyYearbook.com
(myyearbook.com)

I interviewed MyYearbook.com co-founder Catherine Cook for a book I wrote in 2008 titled *Principles of Internet Marketing*, and found myself fascinated by how honed in she was on the needs of her generation. Set-up for the high school crowd, MyYearbook.com has grown up with its audience, and, with millions of active members, is a fun way for Millenials to connect.

BrazenCareerist.com
(brazencareerist.com)

A blog-oriented network, BrazenCareerist.com seems a bit smarter than the average Gen-Y targeted network. It's a place for members to write their own blog posts that get broadcasted by other community members, potentially leading to some pretty high exposure.

20 Something Bloggers
(20sb.net)

If you've never heard of Ning, it's an online resource where anybody can create a social network of their own, under any topic. Well, 20 Something Bloggers is a pretty good one for Gen Y members, letting them connect through online chatrooms, blogs, groups, and other resources.

General Networking Sites

If you have a specific interest, then there's a network for it. It would clearly be impossible to list all of the great sites for each and every area of interest. But along with Facebook, there are other broad-based sites that are worth looking into.

hi5

(hi5.com)

In terms of media attention, hi5 is often overshadowed by its larger competitor, Facebook. But as it closes in on 100 million members, hi5 is a networking force to be reckoned with. Plenty of opportunities here to meet with all sorts of people.

Bebo

(bebo.com)

Owned by AOL, Bebo enjoys a lot of popularity in the UK and is quickly picking up steam in the US and in other parts of the world.

Friendster

(friendster.com)

One of the early entrants in the social media space, Friendster never quite picked up the same steam as rivals MySpace and later Facebook. But, with its popularity in Asia reaching new heights, it's poised to start gaining more attention in the US. Good interface makes it easy to use and market yourself.

APPENDIX E

NETWORKING EVENTS

As important as online networking efforts will be in your self-promotional efforts, it's going to be just as important to get out from behind your computer and network in the real world. It's important to look people in the eye, shake hands, have an in-person conversation and walk away with a business card and an expectation to re-connect again in the future. Nothing can quite replace the power of a face-to-face meeting. The problem is finding the right events to go to.

As I had mentioned earlier in the book, you can find some networking events by going online or by asking the opinions of friends and co-workers in and around your area of interest. To make it even easier, I've assembled the following list of organizations that manage events or provide information on events within different geographies and for different areas of interest. You'll be able to find this list in the Resources page of my blog at jaymiletsky.com.

Networking Event Finders

http://networkingeventfinders.com/

This site by high quality event managers allows you to find events according to geography. It also provides some good blogs and tips for how to network yourself better.

NetParty

http://www.netparty.com/

Perfect for the young, hip professional, NetParty hold events in bars and lounges, mixing a party type of atmosphere, music, and dancing with opportunities to meet other like-minded professionals. Find an event by location—you'll meet plenty of people to career-connect with, and who knows—in this environment you may even score a date!

Networking For Professionals (NFP)

http://networkingforprofessionals.com/

This site allows you to find events by geography and date. They run some pretty good events with active participants who are passionate about meeting people. NFP also runs off-beat events, such as "high speed networking", which is like speed dating, but rather than making romantic connections, you get to interact rapid-fire style with other professional networkers.

eWomen Network

http://www.ewomennetwork.com

For women interested in networking with other women, this organization gives great access to connect professionally with like-minded women.

Event Mingle

http://www.eventmingle.com

A central source for people and organizations that want to host an event, Event Mingle not only helps organizers create better events, but they can provide you with a robust list of networking events, conferences, and trade shows that you could benefit from attending.

M&C (Meetings and Conventions)

http://www.mcmag.com

If you visit this site, you'll find a good amount of info that you probably won't need, but check out their event calendar and you'll find a list of upcoming events in practically every major city (and not so major ones), across all sorts of industries. You won't find a lot of events taking place in bars and clubs, but you'll find some great shows in major conference centers.

MeetUp.com

http://www.meetup.com

Hands-down one of the best resources for finding an offline event, MeetUp.com lets you join any number of member-created groups formed around absolutely any interest. Some groups are better than others, but the ones that are serious and well-run will likely have regularly scheduled meetings with lots of chances to meet new people.

Speednetworking.com

http://www.speednetworking.com/

Another speed-dating inspired site, Speednetworking.com brings people together in a high-speed setting where you're guaranteed to meet a large number of people in a relatively short period of time. It feels a little cheesy at first, but it's kind of a fun way to get to know people without getting locked into a long conversation with any one person.

Event Brite

http://www.eventbrite.com

Event Brite provides you with a little bit of everything, acting as a resource for any person or organization that wants to host an event. Visit this site and you'll find all sorts of classes, seminars, and events in practically any topic and any area of the country.

APPENDIX F

STRATEGIES FOR SUCCESS

Successful people apply a number of positive strategies in their quest to achieve the most they can in all they do. Some of these strategies (time management, organization, stress reduction, lifelong learning, positive character traits, and so on) were explained in previous chapters. Some of the strategies people apply are specific to a particular field (such as learning a specialized skill or language) or involve developing or perfecting personal skills (such as problem-solving skills, gathering and analyzing data, and the like).

To succeed in your career, you must constantly improve yourself and your standing within your company. To be considered for promotion (or simply to make yourself a valued employee worth keeping in times of downsizing), you must master the tasks your company requires of employees in high-level positions. Do this by (1) establishing your goal for advancement, (2) learning what is required to reach the goal, (3) developing and implementing a plan of action, (4) persisting with an optimistic purpose and clear sense of direction, and (5) committing the time and effort required to reach your advancement potential.

Success strategies in this chapter include being clear about what you want and visualizing it to obtain it. Tips are presented for becoming and remaining a professional in all you do and say as well as in the image you project. Becoming an expert in your field and demonstrating integrity are ways to open up advancement opportunities for yourself.

1: Visualize Success

You must first have a clear picture in your mind of what a successful career looks like to you. Be specific about what you want to do and the position you want to attain. For instance, imagine sitting in your future office carrying out your duties. What does your office look like? Is there a nameplate on your desk? Visualize the title under your name. What specific tasks are you performing?

Make your visualization as clear and detailed as possible. Feel the self-confidence and excitement as you work. Take things further and see what you are wearing and how you feel accomplishing your new duties. See the faces of people who report to you. Are they happy and confident? Are you satisfied with their work and how your leadership skills influence their attitudes and affect their job?

Be Clear about Your Vision

People have vastly different ideas about what success means to them. The more specific you are in your personal definition of success, the more clearly you will be able to visualize yourself achieving a positive outcome.

Because defining your career aspirations enables you to set meaningful goals, it is necessary to pinpoint exactly what you hope to achieve. Make the connection between where you are and where you want to be by visualizing how you will look, feel, and act when you reach your goals. Do you hope to take on additional challenging responsibilities with confidence? If so, imagine how it feels to be confident. When you receive a promotion, how will you carry out your responsibilities, speak to subordinates, solve problems, and participate in management brain-storming sessions? See yourself effectively performing each of these activities.

You will enrich your visualizations by attaching significant meaning and emotion to them. Make the most of your visualizations to accomplish a task or to win a promotion in much the same way an athlete visualizes winning a competition.

- When you have to give a presentation, see yourself skillfully delivering your message over and over to perfection. Picture the attentive, receptive audience receiving your message with interest.

- If you have to train someone, imagine a flawless training session where you present every detail with clear direction. See the trainee listening to you and understanding your directives.

- Visualize positive outcomes to decisions you make, tasks you perform, plans you arrange, and ideas you submit.

Using all your senses will make the visualization more realistic and will give you a better chance of achieving the desired result. To feel the emotion in the visualization, think about a time when you experienced the same feeling you want to create in your visualization. For instance, to visualize being self-assured, remember a time when your confidence soared and try to re-create that same feeling. Imitate confident body language—stand straight, move with determination, be energetic. Use positive self-talk; see yourself communicating with other executives; imagine your head is filled with creative ideas and see yourself implementing them.

The next time something wonderful happens to you or you feel a strong positive emotion (such as confidence, high energy, and happiness), pay particular attention to the emotional feelings and physical responses the emotion creates. Then re-create that positive feeling whenever you visualize.

In all ways **see** yourself being successful.

Visualization Activity

Sit in a quiet place where you will not be disturbed. Close your eyes and let your mind get quiet for a few moments. Create this visualization: See yourself sitting at your desk working. Imagine that your boss walks up to you and commends you for doing a superior job. Make his comment to you about a specific task or project you did, not just a general pat on the back for all you do. Perhaps he says, "Your revenue generating idea about the Henderson project was terrific. I'm excited about the very real possibility of a highly profitable second quarter." Hear the sincere praise in his voice. Feel the proud satisfaction run through you as you straighten and accept his compliment with a smile.

Visualize yourself successfully advancing in your company.

2: Learn How to Advance within the Company

Most companies have a particular line of progression, a ladder of success so to speak, when it comes to advancement. Employees must navigate the rungs of this ladder to attain higher positions.

A company's organization chart defines the arrangement of positions that form its line of authority. Specific duties are assigned to people who hold each of these positions. The size of the company and the type of organizational structure determine the number of layers of authority. You might vie for a management position or opt to be a project manager or team leader, depending on how much responsibility you want to assume and your credentials for filling the position you desire.

Find out how many organizational levels your company has and decide which one(s) is best for you. What is the most direct path to the position you would like to have? Is consideration of candidates based on performance? On education? On job experience? On network contacts? How can you get started on your company's advancement path? Visualize yourself stepping out of your comfort zone and working toward the promotion you want.

After you have clearly defined your career ambitions, ask yourself where you might fit in at the management level. What special skills and knowledge do you have that sets you apart from your coworkers? What personal attributes do you have that sets you apart? For what position are you best suited?

Certain standards, requirements, education, and so forth must be met before a person will be considered for a promotion. Meeting these demands is your first step in becoming a serious candidate for a higher level position. Develop your communication skills to an expert level by taking a class, joining a speakers' group, volunteering to give a presentation, etc. Learn how to overcome obstacles that get in your way by brainstorming solutions and creatively applying them. Evaluate your competencies on a regular basis and implement changes in your action plan if needed, such as laying out a schedule to achieve certifications or a degree and breaking down your list into manageable parts. Follow activities through to completion and think about how you can use your new knowledge on your current job.

Explore the options available to you by learning all you can about what it takes to move up through the ranks of your company. Can you arrange a meeting with your boss to discuss your promotional possibilities? Ask him how you can increase your value to the company, as well as let him know what you have accomplished so far. Show you are a person who gets results.

What criteria does your boss use for performance evaluations and promotions? Have him assess your skills and competencies to see how they fit with the requirements of higher-level positions. Ask for feedback on your personal traits and work habits as well.

Can you request from human resources a job description of the next level position for which you are qualified? Are there particular steps you need to take to get that promotion? How many other positions are there for which you are qualified? How often are management level openings filled from within the company? How did the top company leaders rise to their positions? Why have they been successful? Is the path they took a feasible one for you to take?

If your company has a formal policy for performing reviews that includes specific worksheets to be completed by the reviewer, are you permitted to access the worksheet information?

In addition, investigate what is typically required of the people who hold the top positions so that you can be sure that is what you really want. What are their day-to-day responsibilities? What do they spend most of their time doing? What are the biggest problems they face? For instance, are you ready to accept the blame or negative criticism if something goes wrong? Are you willing to accept responsibility for your subordinates' actions without making excuses? Do you have the time and stamina to devote to a management position? Money and titles are not everything, especially if you don't like doing the work involved or if you dislike managing people.

Before you climb the corporate ladder, you should have a clear picture of what the job involves on a daily basis. You want to enjoy your job if you get a promotion. If you do not feel you would enjoy the required work, the promotion you are seeking may not be for you.

Working toward career advancement can consume all of your time. Make sure the personal sacrifice is worth the cost of the advancement, especially when it involves the lives of family members. You need to consider the impact that your long-term commitment to advancement will have on your personal life. You must be willing to spend long hours on the job and less time on your family and personal life.

Ask yourself the following questions to determine whether you have the mindset to pursue a management position.

1. What do you plan to accomplish at your company in the next year? Can you imagine having already accomplished it?

2. What do you want from a job more than anything (i.e., job satisfaction, independence, money, a title, etc.)?

3. Is your goal to perform a routine job and collect a paycheck or to climb the corporate ladder?

4. If you do not aspire to a higher-level position at your present company, how do you expect to achieve personal success in your job?

5. If you do aspire to a higher-level position in your company, what is the specific position you want?

6. What steps will you have to take to attain the position you want?

7. Do you like working hands-on with technology or do you prefer more intellectual, idea generating, and less concrete pursuits?

8. Have you observed how people in the higher-level positions in your company act, dress, and speak, and can you emulate them?

9. Do you know what duties and responsibilities people have in the positions to which you aspire, and are you willing to do them?

10. Do you have the necessary background and education to rise to the position you would like to have?

11. Can you relate your past accomplishments and experiences to the requirements for a management position in your company?

12. Do you prefer using a variety of skills and doing a multitude of tasks on the job?

13. Do you crave the excitement of tackling high-level problems and can you manage the stress that goes with it?

14. Do you have a high degree of time and energy that you are willing to expend on the job?

15. Do you like using creativity and innovation to solve problems?

16. Do you like working with a diverse group of people?

17. Can you see yourself persuading, leading, and supervising others? Are you prepared for the responsibility that goes with those duties?

18. Do you like facing significant challenges and problems?

19. Can you see yourself calmly and objectively handling crisis situations?

20. Are you committed enough to follow through on every duty and decision?

21. Can you handle the responsibilities and pressures of a management position?

22. Are you decisive?

23. Can you take on more responsibility in your current position to prepare for a higher-level position?

24. Are you a self-starter?

25. Do you finish what you start in a timely manner?

26. Do you keep your skills and knowledge updated?

27. Do you have excellent communication and interpersonal skills?

28. Are you willing to accept complete responsibility for your actions?

29. Are you willing to be held accountable for your subordinates' actions?

30. Do you do your best work all the time?

The first seven questions will require an in-depth answer according to your goals. Questions 8 through 30 should be answered with yes if you are serious about accepting a management position.

Talk to people who are in positions to which you aspire. What did they do to achieve promotions? Ask them to describe their background and credentials. Do you have similar credentials? Do you have the passion and commitment that they have for their positions?

Be sure to let your boss or human resource manager know you are interested in a promotion or a different position in the company with more responsibility. Even if you believe you are qualified for or are the next person in line for a position, without expressly stating your intentions, you may be passed over for the promotion. Management may feel you are content in your current position and not interested in changing. Often if a specific position is available, because of legal or union polices, HR will be required to post the opening, solicit resumes, and interview candidates. Keep your resume updated at all times so you are prepared to go through the proper promotion procedures. In addition, others in your company may be hoping to move up into the position you want. This competition can wreak havoc on coworker relationships. You may want to develop strategies for dealing with this competition such as discussing your intentions with coworkers and wishing others well in their pursuits.

Make sure you are qualified for a management position—take on additional projects, volunteer for committees, become self-directed, be professional at all times, and attend workshops or classes related to the duties required of higher positions.

Often people do not advance in a company through promotions. Their advancement may result via a title change or other recognition, newly defined tasks, a bonus, flextime, a better work environment (like a new office or a technology upgrade), or more challenging responsibilities and the freedom to work independently.

If you cannot advance the way you would like within your company (i.e., no upward positions to seek; no raises available), you may have to get into the mindset of doing your best where you are or else consider looking for other employment more suited to your ambitions.

TIP Follow the most direct path to the position you want.

3: Be a Representative for Excellence

Demonstrate integrity and live by the highest code of ethics in everything you do every day; you will be judged by the standards you set for yourself. Make it a habit to produce impeccable work.

Challenge yourself in all ways. Instead of meeting deadlines, exceed them. After completing your duties, take on more responsibility. During brainstorming sessions, contribute ideas. Prove yourself by figuring out effective ways to contribute to the company's bottom line and let management know how the company has benefited from your ideas. Be a results-oriented person who delivers quality and value and integrates creative solutions.

Your professional image and attitude is projected through your actions, speech, and appearance.

Tips for Projecting an Effective Professional Image

- Discipline yourself to be positive and enthusiastic.
- In tense situations choose positive responses by maintaining perspective and getting along well with others.
- Acknowledge mistakes and shortcomings and learn how to correct them.
- Develop a reputation for being a resourceful problem solver.
- Leverage your strengths and expertise to have maximum impact on the decisions you make.
- Be organized, efficient, flexible, and self-motivated.
- Master your tasks and fully expand your area of expertise so that you can boost your output.
- Keep up with the latest developments in your company and in your field.
- Cultivate unique talents that give you a definite edge.
- Gain visibility by taking the kind of action that will propel you into the sights of management personnel.

- Be proactive, implement time- and money-saving procedures, and take appropriate risks.

- Have a vision—a mapped plan for your career that includes key components to keep your career moving in the right direction.

- Think of change as an opportunity that leaves you open to new methods of performance.

- Grow and change to meet new challenges.

- Never let complacency set in or allow your skills to become obsolete.

- Learn as much as you can about the company for which you work so that you can identify the best ways to contribute to its success.

- Be a positive role model.

TIP Demonstrate integrity and ethics in all you do.

4: Become an Expert at Your Job

An expert is one who excels at what he or she does, someone who is a skilled authority figure—a professional in every sense. Experts are valuable assets and resources to their employers. How do you become an expert at your job? You become an expert by being someone who not only has valuable skills but also has a higher-than-average performance level. Experts do their best at all times, exceeding expectations in most cases. They are excited about and invested in their work. They do not simply want to get ahead; they want to enjoy their work. Job satisfaction is as important to them as advancement.

Experts achieve extraordinary results built on a solid foundation of knowledge that they continuously update. They have an in-depth understanding of their capabilities and talents and know where to develop new, essential competencies as they are needed. They are creative thinkers, competent decision-makers, and expend the maximum effort to tackle tasks and responsibilities. While maintaining a record of solid performance and productivity, experts increase their learning by engaging in significant projects that test their knowledge and incorporate their skills.

Experts are lifelong learners who enjoy broadening their knowledge base, integrating new ways of doing tasks, and keeping up with cutting-edge technology and research. They continually question strategies and methods that are in use, experiment with new concepts, overcome adversity, and collaborate with others. All of this takes a great deal of self-discipline. This self-discipline will help you:

- Keep emotions in check
- Devote the required time to work extra hours and learn crucial skills and knowledge
- Keep going through discouragement
- Meet challenges head on
- Avoid complacency and procrastination
- Stay organized
- Work toward goals

An expert's word carries a high degree of weight throughout her company and industry because she learns what needs to be done, and she gets it done. Being an expert is a great boost to her job security as the company will likely do everything it can to keep its experts. In addition to being on top of their game at their companies, experts keep abreast of what competitors are doing so they are not blindsided by the competition.

TIP Excel at all you do and exceed expectations.

5: Keep a Record of Your Accomplishments

Many job seekers put together a portfolio to take on job interviews. Established employees should also assemble a portfolio of tangible examples of their on-the-job accomplishments, including significant achievements, training documents and certifications, awards and other types of recognition, outstanding performance reviews, and the like. In short, anything that shows what you have done well and are capable of doing should be included in your work portfolio.

Be sure to add documentation for attendance at seminars, conferences, and college courses; articles you have published; and any press coverage you have enjoyed. You might also include a brief description of significant projects you handled, an inventory of your competencies, a graph of figures that measure procedures that you streamlined, and outcomes that saved your company money or increased its profits. Any time you successfully complete tasks and projects that go beyond your job description, include a sample or description of them in your portfolio. However, do not take copies of company documents without permission.

Always keep an updated resume and list of references, as well as current letters of recommendation, in your portfolio.

 TIP   Assemble a portfolio of on-the-job accomplishments.

6: Find a Mentor

A mentor or coach can provide invaluable counsel throughout your career. Select someone in a high-level management position whose work you respect and who is willing to be your mentor. By aligning yourself with an individual who is talented and highly regarded by management, you will have an inside track to progress through the ranks of your company. This relationship can also give you a different perspective of management-level work.

A management-level mentor is someone you can bounce ideas off, ask for specific career advice, and brainstorm ways to increase your visibility in the company. She can help you see where your position and every other one fits into the big picture, giving you an overall understanding of company operations. She can help you decide what position you would like and how to advance to it. This information could also alert you to a host of available options you didn't already consider.

A mentor can expand your area of expertise by offering her seasoned experience and knowledge; by identifying areas you need to develop; and by pointing out ways to correct problem areas with your skills, knowledge, and personal traits. She can identify opportunities, revealing possibilities that you may not have previously considered. This guidance leads to a broader understanding of your competencies and how they fit into the company's management positions.

Your mentor should be someone you can get along with, confidently accept feedback from, and trust implicitly to help you succeed.

Find a mentor in a high-level management position.

7: Write a Training Manual

Write a training manual for your position if there isn't one already available. The training manual should include a complete description of every one of your duties and the procedures for completing those duties. Be sure to finish assigned work before taking on a training manual project. Check your company's policies and get appropriate permission. If a manual exists, be sure it is accurate and current; otherwise, update it.

The training manual should be written in clear, simple-to-understand language. Reduce the explanation for each task to a step-by-step process if possible. Doing so will make it easy for someone to take over if you leave your position. If you are promoted, the manual will not only showcase your ability to communicate and compile directions, but also be a timesaver when training a replacement, which may fall to you.

Keep your training manual up to date. As your software programs and technology change and methods become outdated, make the appropriate changes. It may be a good idea to update the manual on a periodic basis.

Write a training manual and keep it updated.

8: Dress the Part

Each work environment has its own dress culture, and you should wear clothing suitable for that particular environment if you want to fit in and be promoted. Whether you like it or not, people judge you by the way you dress.

If your company has a dress code, adhere to it. If it does not, dress appropriately for the business. Dressing a step above your current position will give others the impression you are a serious, upwardly mobile professional. To enhance your professional image, observe the way people dress in upper-management positions and imitate their style. There is generally a distinction in the way management-level professionals dress as compared to their subordinates. For example, consider how the following bank employees might dress: a teller, a loan officer, a finance officer, and a bank president. Their dress would probably become more professional looking as their rank increased. Look at the chain of command in your company and come up with a similar example of how employees dress from entry-level jobs to top management.

No matter how you dress, business casual or professional, your clothing should be impeccable. You do not have to spend a fortune on your wardrobe, but you should wear clothing that fits well, looks good on you, shows you are serious about your work, and is spotless and pressed. Dress all the way to your toes, keeping shoes polished and in good repair.

Jewelry, belts, ties, and other accessories should be appropriate for your outfit and the circumstances. For example, avoid wearing clunky, noisy bracelets; ties with cartoon characters; flip-flops; and similar dress faux pas if you aspire to an upper management position.

TIP People judge you by the way you dress; be professional.

9: Network

Networking is a means for you to exchange information, learn from and help others, and discover new opportunities. Build your network inside and outside of your company by including supervisors, coworkers, customers, members of organizations to which you belong, and personal friends. Actively cultivate these relationships. Look for opportunities to reconnect with people with whom you have not recently spoken.

Become an extrovert when it comes to networking by approaching people outside of your normal environment, such as while attending conferences and professional meetings and events. Introduce yourself and briefly talk about your profession and expertise. Exchange business cards with people who would be valuable additions to your network.

Joining a professional organization in your field shows you are serious about your career and provides you important contacts. Become an active member by attending meetings and volunteering for committees, which will increase your visibility, develop your social skills, and demonstrate your leadership abilities. In addition, your contribution can have a significant impact on the organization's goals. Keep up with the latest industry news so that you can discuss new methods and technology, company expansions and downsizing, individuals who hold top positions in companies, etc., with other members. You can learn about professional organizations in your field by researching online, asking coworkers, or contacting your local library or Chamber of Commerce.

Join one or more of the many professional and social networks on the Internet (i.e., LinkedIn, Facebook, Twitter, etc.) to take advantage of the information provided by these sites and the professionals who have joined them.

Read blogs related to your field or area of expertise or start a professional blog of your own.

 TIP Build a solid network.

Summary

Utilize positive personal and professional strategies, such as developing expert-level skills and problem-solving abilities, to help you attain career success. Create a clear visual of your ideal job. See yourself performing your duties, contributing ideas, and managing your staff. Picture yourself successfully completing your tasks and dealing with people.

Learn how to advance within your company by finding out what specifically you must do to join the management team. Define your special abilities, knowledge, and credentials so that you can explore management options. Talk to your supervisor and human resource personnel to learn as much as you can about the current available positions. Observe supervisors and emulate their traits and expertise. Find a mentor to help you develop an action plan and advise you on proper protocol. Remember the merits of job satisfaction when seeking advancement.

Challenge and discipline yourself to be a representative for excellence by producing impeccable work at all times. Maintain a positive attitude, be organized and efficient, and keep up with the latest developments in your field and with technology advances. Master your present tasks; become a talented expert with a broad knowledge base. Consider the sacrifices you will have to make in your personal life in order to commit to a major job promotion and to develop a career. Build a portfolio of on-the-job accomplishments to showcase your talents and achievements. In addition, write a training manual for completing your current duties so that someone else can be adequately trained when you are promoted. Build a solid network of supervisors, colleagues, customers, friends, and acquaintances.

INDEX

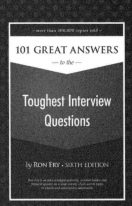